A PLUME BOOK

YOU DON'T HA

Virginia Ahern

ALIDA NUGENT currently resides in Brooklyn, where she gets dark lipstick on her bagels and tries to find dive bars that serve dirty martinis. She is also the author of *Don't Worry, It Gets Worse*.

Praise for *Don't Worry, It Gets Worse*

"Reading *Don't Worry, It Gets Worse* is the equivalent of spending an evening out with your funniest friend. Nugent keeps you laughing from start to finish—even her asides are gems."

—Rachel Dratch, *Saturday Night Live* cast member (1996–2007) and author of *Girl Walks into a Bar . . .*

"Charming. . . . Nugent is a confection of fabulosity, a sharp and hilarious mind that falls a little bit in love—and a little bit in hate—with the ridiculous world around her. Her observations on post-collegiate life are somehow both cutting and warm, and all the more wonderful for it."

—Sara Barron, author of *People Are Unappealing: Even Me*

"Nugent's voice comes across as loyal and tough, and her sense of humor and authenticity will appeal to readers going through related chapters in their own post-college lives. This book, like one of its myriad cocktails, is dry, dirty, and surprisingly refreshing."
—*Kirkus Reviews*

"If Liz Lemon's younger sister existed, she'd be just like Alida Nugent: a little bit awkward, perpetually single, and defiantly weird."
—*Book Riot*

"[Nugent's] essays are warm, funny slices of postcollegiate life, including amusing and helpful bits of advice from a very real person."
—*Time Out New York*

"Honest, real, and hilarious."
—*Shelf Awareness*

"Humorous . . . [with] wickedly crafted insights."
—*New York Journal of Books*

"Painfully hilarious, eye-opening, and breathtakingly well-written. Nugent is a force to be reckoned with. . . . We'll be hearing from her for years to come."
—*Dish Magazine*

"Depressingly realistic and hilariously offbeat. . . . Nugent is not afraid to tell the truth, no matter how ugly it gets."
—*Brooklyn Daily Eagle*

You Don't Have to Like Me

*Essays on
Growing Up, Speaking Out,
and Finding Feminism*

Alida Nugent

A PLUME BOOK

PLUME
An imprint of Penguin Random House LLC
375 Hudson Street
New York, New York 10014
penguin.com

LIBRARY OF CONGRESS CATALOGING-IN-PUBLICATION DATA
Nugent, Alida.
    You don't have to like me : essays on growing up, speaking out, and finding feminism / Alida Nugent. — First Edition.
        pages cm
    ISBN 978-0-142-18168-3 (paperback)
    1. Feminism—Humor. I. Title.
    PN6231.F44N84 2015
    814'.6—dc23   2015016560

Printed in the United States of America
10 9 8 7 6 5 4 3 2 1

I had no second thoughts in dedicating this to my father. You passed along your love of books to me, and with that love you gave me more worlds than I ever could have imagined. Thanks for always believing in me and for sometimes letting me sit in your armchair.

Contents

Introduction

It's an unseasonably warm winter morning, and I am in a good mood. The first thing I see when I arrive at work, twenty minutes late, is an e-mail. The subject line reads "Be Safe," and it is e-addressed to three of my girlfriends.

"Hey," it begins. Innocuous start. I am intrigued because the last time this friend sent me an e-mail, it was about paying her forty dollars for an all-you-can-drink brunch in Lower Manhattan.

"Looks like there was an attempted assault in your neighborhood." I nod slowly and sip my coffee, like *go on, you have my attention*. "Just be extra vigilant." It ends with a news link, as proof. I click it.

A man pushed a woman down to the ground while she was walking on the same block on which I buy my eggs, and she was now in the hospital. I think about myself on that block, hands full with bags of chips, Brie, and diet ginger ale.

The woman would be fine, the article said, but her attacker had gotten away. The police released a description whose sole detail was the fact that the man "wore a sweatshirt." The comments in the article were about how stupid the woman was for walking home so late. Again, I think about myself, walking home tipsy from two-martini happy hour. I think about two a.m., when I don't have enough money in my wallet for a cab. I think about risk.

My friend Caroline responds to this e-mail first. "I walk that way a lot. This makes me VERY NERVOUS." For once, I don't find the caps overkill.

I pitch in next: "Guess it's good I already hold my keys like they're Wolverine claws!" I add a little humor to mask what I really want to say: "I'm always afraid of walking alone at night." "Do we have to be worried everywhere we go?" And, of course:

"It could have been me."

I have this thought all too frequently, not just when something happens on my block, or in Brooklyn, or in New York. It's because this type of story is unavoidable anywhere you are. Every time you read the news or turn on the TV, it's like some sort of monstrous Groundhog Day: assaults that happen to women on a college campus, or on a street, or in the house of someone they trusted, or while on a jog around the neighborhood. And every day, we read these stories silently, at our desks or on our phones, finding reasons why it wouldn't have been us.

Well, I don't really walk home that late. I usually take a cab. I try not to get too drunk. I try not to take drinks from other people. I am so good at following my gut. I am so vigilant. I look behind me, even when I'm wearing headphones.

But still, we know the truth. We know that it could always, *always*, be us. Or it was us. Or it was our best friend, or sister, or roommate. We know that walking late could be six p.m. or one a.m. We know that our gut is sometimes wrong. We know that we like to drink, and have fun, and meet new people. We know that we can always be wrong about the people we let our guard down around. We know why we are always scared.

So, to make us feel safer, we give each other tips.

Women are full of tips. There are good tips, like which translucent powder to use and how to find the right shapewear for particular dresses. There are recommendations of cheap yoga places and lunch spots and lemony olive oil. There are other tips—never leave your drink unattended, give your friends the address of the restaurant where you're meeting that guy—that are more about preserving life than hairstyles. Both are normal and needed.

At the very least, these tips serve to remind me how completely absurd it is to be a woman these days. In the same GChat conversation, you can talk about the best way to use a curling iron and whether pepper spray is legal in your state. The answer is to curl some pieces of hair toward your face and other pieces away from your face, and in New York State, at least, it is legal but has restrictions. Or you might talk about the best shows to watch on Netflix when you are hungover, followed by how to turn down a drink in a way that is both nice and assertive enough to end the conversation. The answer to this is *Gilmore Girls*, and that you are going sober for your boyfriend, *Fast and Furious* franchise star Vin Diesel.

I should point out that these frustrating ironies of modern womanhood don't affect how much I love being a woman. When I wear the suggested powder and it doesn't fade *all day*, and I come home with a porcelain-doll face with no creases or oil slicks, I feel on top of the world. When I get to dance to "All the Single Ladies," or have a girls' night out where I shovel goat cheese salads into my face, or read about other greater women like Malala Yousafzai, I'm pretty thrilled to be a woman. However, with these triumphs comes the reminder that women have only been able to vote in the United States for less than one hundred years, or that in 2010, two-thirds of the world's illiterate were women, or, according to RAINN (Rape, Abuse and Incest National Network), a woman is sexually assaulted every 107 seconds. So. The world feels less like "how lovely to be a woman!" and more like "being a woman is objectively hard in the scheme of things!"

The night of the e-mail chain, I had to walk down that same street where the woman was jumped. On that short walk home, I was reminded of how much more real my fear of the dark is, now that I am older. Each time I step off the subway and make the five-minute walk to my door, I feel nervous. I look for safety points that put my mind at ease. People with baby carriages, couples, streetlights, open stores, and other women. I find myself behind a shadowy figure who turns sharply at the sound of my boot heels approaching. She is a pretty Asian girl in absolutely stellar maroon pants. Both of us relax and half-smile when our eyes meet. We are relieved. We continue walking in a distant single file, feeling the safety in numbers.

I think about her, my friends, my roommate waiting for me when I close the door behind me, and all the women in my life who send me e-mails and give me tips. We are each other's relief in a world where relief is hard to come by.

It took me a long time to call myself a feminist. It took me an even longer time to say it out loud. And after that happened, I had to start explaining myself to people. A lot. This can be fun if you're the type of person who, every once in a while, likes it when people tell you to your face why they think you're an idiot.

Calling yourself a feminist is like making a comment on the Internet in real life: there's always somebody who is going to disagree with your beliefs, and that person is going to express this disagreement with great passion and little digs at your life choices. Some people won't like you as much anymore. You will be uncomfortable and end up learning nasty truths about some people you thought you respected. Believe me: I've dropped the f-bomb at parties, when I've mistaken two glasses of whiskey for comfort. Rookie mistake! Parties are awful and you should never be comfortable at them. And if you are looking for a surefire way to turn a comfortable party into a very alcohol-fueled romp through gender politics, bring up feminism.

It happens the same way pretty much every time. I'll be in a conversation with a group of people about something topical. *These people seem pretty cool*, I think. One of them has a nose ring, which has been on my cool barometer since 1992. Then, I wave my crudité around and say something like, "Well, as a feminist, I think that . . ." and . . . give it, like, three seconds. Sometimes the convo will go well. Sometimes people will go "tell me more," and we will pour more wine into mismatched cups and talk about street harassment. But *usually* . . .

"Whoa, whoa a *feminist*!" A guy will shake his hands at me in mock fear, as though I will perhaps suddenly get on a soapbox and pour menstrual blood all over him in protest.

Inevitably, this is followed by: "So, why are you a feminist?" I used to open my mouth immediately after this question but now I wait *juuuust* a millisecond for the inevitable fallout.

"I get that men and women should be equal, man, but you guys just have such a bad rep! You don't want women and men to be *equal*, you want women to be BETTER, right?"

Well. If you are worried about the effects of feminism and you are a man, it's probably because you are worried that *men* will start to be treated like *women* have been treated since the dawn of time. By this I mean worse, which makes you nervous, no doubt. Now burn me! Burn me at the stake like the witch that I am!

Every once in a while another woman joins in: "Oh, I'm not a feminist. I believe in some of the things feminism stands for, but I'm not nearly that extreme," as though the concept of equality is as Xtreme as pulling off a snowboard trick while drinking a Mountain Dew on a real mountain.

When a *woman* says she's not a feminist, I always get a little thrown off guard. It's literally *for her.* But, instead, I hear this:

"Oh, I don't like to call myself a feminist—I love men!"

Yes. Okay. Men are great. They smell good. They play baseball in stadiums that have good hamburgers and beer. I have no qualms with many of the men in the world! I only have qualms with men who call me babe in casual conversation, men who sit with their legs spread on the subway, and men who think that being good at football means you are allowed to kill people. Anyway, what I'm saying is that you can love men if you want to. You can feel however you want about them. Equality has nothing to do with loving or hating them. And it has *everything* to do with feminism.

I think there are usually two reasons why women say they aren't feminists. One is because they don't know what it means. The other is because they want to be liked by people. I get this. I generally love being liked, especially by friends' parents, cute old people, and every dog I encounter. As women, we place a lot of stock into being liked. We are *supposed* to be liked, and agreeable, and demure. We aren't supposed to be disruptive. Saying you are a feminist means you want more. Women and Oliver Twist should never want more! It's not ladylike (or orphanlike). We are supposed to be happy. Say yes. Nod along. The truth is, most of the time, women don't want to publicly declare themselves feminists because of good old-fashioned not-interested-in-going-there syndrome. Feminism, after all, is a very unlikable word. Feminism is standing behind you, screaming that your body hair needs to grow out. Feminism is yelling at all your favorite men, calling them disgusting and spitting at their genitals. Feminism is rude!

This, of course, is wrong. Very wrong. I'm talking Crocs when it's raining, people who are sure that Dumbledore will make it through *Harry Potter* alive, and those who think it's appropriate to leave less than a 15 percent tip at dinner wrong. Feminism isn't wrong. Feminism is important.

And that's why I'm writing this book. For years, I treaded lightly around the word because I didn't want to deal with people's reactions. I worried about being liked more than I worried about being right, or tough, or honest. I made a living as a blogger, and then as an author, and I still feared saying it. I mean, I wrote publicly about how sex was like throwing an octopus against the wall and yet here I was, unable to utter the word. I was a real human woman who could really benefit from the declaration, and I was still afraid. Then, after I got tired of a great many things, I got a lot more scared of my disadvantages than the actual word "feminism."

Whenever I hear feminism defined, I sometimes want to go all *Princess Bride* on their ass: "No, no, no. I do not think you know what that word means." Given that so many graduation speeches begin with *"Merriam-Webster's Dictionary* defines

'blank' as . . . ," you'd think people would look up the definition of feminism more often. But, instead, we get a bunch of
half-assed sloppy explanations that come down to stereotypes
and fear. If you've taken any gender studies classes, this might
be a bit repetitive but it always bears repeating:

**Feminism: the theory of the political, economic, and so-
cial equality of the sexes.**

You see that? Equality! A novel concept! You see, the true
definition of feminism is not

- eating men for supper with fava beans and a nice
  Chianti;
- shipping men off to a remote island and making
  them fight each other for our entertainment, like the
  Hunger Games but with less kid death;
- shunning women who choose to do traditional,
  old-fashioned things like "cook dinner" or "raise a
  baby" or "like men";
- yelling at men for doing real caveman stuff like
  opening the door or helping us with the groceries;
- telling you how to be a woman.

When it is at its best, feminism points out problematic men
and women and problematic behavior. It tells women that they
are allowed to take control over their own bodies, what they
look like, and whom they have sex with. It points out what is
wrong with the world. It points out the ugly. It points out the
frightening. It points out that women are mistreated often,
both in tangible and intangible ways. It talks about difficult
things that need addressing. It shines bright lights into society,
into the world, and right smack into your damn party. The
hard truth is this: we all know women and men aren't treated

equally across the world. We can Google this in two seconds and find real statistics about these differences, easily. So, the truth is this: if you are not a feminist because you believe *you* have it good, you're saying, "I have all I need, and I don't care that other women don't."

The point is, you need to be willing to *go there.*

To me, feminism means getting a fair shot. It doesn't mean taking things away from other people. It doesn't mean the death of men. It means that in the grand scheme of humanity, it doesn't make sense that women aren't treated as human as other humans. It means that all the women in your life deserve the careers they want, and they deserve to be compensated equally. It means that people will be held accountable for sexual assault. It means that women will be looked at as decision makers. It means that women will feel like their own bodies belong to them. It's not man-hating. It just means we no longer want to put up with bullshit, and with every girl who is told she's "asking for it," our bullshit tolerance is getting lower and lower. It's all sensible adjustments to culture—I don't expect women to become Amazonian warriors à la *Mad Max.* They will not be trotting down the streets, spearing white men in suits. They will simply be an equal part of the conversation. Equality is the key word. If I give a dollar and ask for change, you get four quarters and not three. The same. SAME.

There's another thing that I believe rounds out the definition: choice. Feminism is fighting for the choice to make informed decisions about your life and body.

There's no right or wrong way to be a woman or to approach being a woman. Yet, somehow, you've probably spent a good part of your life thinking about the rules that come with being a woman: get a period, want children, want men, shave your legs and thighs and all the hair below your neck. Feminism is saying "choose how you want to live your life in ways that are right for you." Wear cat eyeliner! Become a burlesque dancer! Shave only one leg! Have six kids and live in a remodeled farmhouse! Get the dessert! Make choices about yourself instead of following all the rules, and abandon the notion that you need to follow any path in order to be a "real woman!" This even has an added benefit for men, because it allows *them* to make choices, too. Want to be a stay-at-home dad? Paint your nails? Lotion your dry skin without losing man points, or whatever? Go for it!

So why are people so scared of it? What's so scary about equality and choice?

Because it means some change to things as we know it. Because it means we admit faults. It means adjustments. And you know what?

It's already starting.

Listen, there are always going to be lecherous, stubborn people who believe that everything I am saying is crap. They won't like me, and they won't like you for calling yourself a feminist. They will work hard to say that feminism destroys all the good things about society—good women, chivalrous men, and gender roles that balance out the world. They will say that catcalling is a compliment, and sexual assault has been blurred to such a gray area they are afraid to even *approach women.*

They say this because they know things are changing. Change is *already happening*, and these people are afraid of being left behind. Women are voicing their fears, their outrage, and they're *teaching* people about it. It's not enough, but we're getting there.

Does feminism still sound scary to you? Is it because it's such a hard *f* sound? Sometimes, I blame the bad wrap for the word on the hard *f* sound, as a lot of unpleasant words begin the same way: fungus, fraternity, finals, felony, and fedora come to mind. I'm going to take a shot in the dark here and say you might be a feminist, too. Now look, I know you might be a little nervous to join us, lest you be ostracized from society and forced to only listen to folk music, but I am here to convince you that it's okay and absolutely essential to say you are a feminist. To other human beings, even! I want you to look those party poopers in the eye and say, "I am a feminist" (and before they open their mouths) "because I believe in making women equal to other humans, like men. I am not here to take all the things. I am here to take what is mine, too. I am a feminist, hear me roar at a normal level, right before I get back to work!"

Not entirely sold if you are a feminist or not? Take my handy quiz:

1. Do you think that your mother should be screamed at on the street on account of how good she looks in her outfit?
2. With your knowledge of both science and anatomy, do you think that women are not humans?
3. Are you an asshole?

If you said no to all three, congratulations! You are a feminist. It's obviously not as simple as this, but hell, it's a good start.

This book isn't a guide to being a female, because I don't think there should be any guidebook for that. Women come in too many shapes and forms. There is no one experience, no birthright, no singular way to identify as a woman. It's just my experiences—I'm sure you will find some similarities and some differences in our lives, none of which make you any more or less a woman than me. I am, however, going to tell you how I grew up to be a feminist, how I learned to speak out, and how I finally stopped caring so much about being liked. It only took me, oh, a bunch of mistakes, a lot of holding my tongue, a long overdue trust in my strength, a hearty "That's ENOUGH," and two whole decades.

Here's to hoping you get there much faster than I did.

You Don't
Have to Like Me

"It's a Girl!"

When someone announces she is pregnant, a number of questions are thrown her way: *What is a soft cheese and why can't you eat it? Do you miss alcohol? Have you heard of our Lord and Savior Jesus Christ? Can I somehow avoid giving you my seat on the subway while still maintaining that I am a good person?* (NO.) *Are you worried it's going to pop out of you like an alien? Do you miss sushi?* And, of course, the classic, *Do you want a boy or a girl?*

The last question is pretty loaded. Usually, the stock answer is "I just hope the baby is healthy," which is understandable. But there are people out there who make their preferred sex known. Sometimes it's a button-upped conservative chiming in with "I've always wanted a *son to carry on the family name,*" like perhaps son is code for "cisgendered, heterosexual, tobacco-chewin' American male." Other times, a Real Housewife–type will comment, "I just want a daughter to deck out in Chanel onesies." However they phrase it, I think people have deeper feelings about this than they are letting on. The real question is this: what battles are you prepared to handle?

Raising a son is quite a task if you want him to be the kind of man who is worth his salt in suits. If your son is white, you might have an easier time with this. If your son isn't, you have to teach him a lot of different rules. If your son is gay? Turn off Fox News; do not collect two hundred dollars. Either way, you have to teach him the ins and outs of being powerful, you have to teach him respect and consent, and you should hopefully teach him that being "a man" can mean showing emotion, crying at movies if he feels like it, and generally being an honest, hardworking, understanding human.

Raising a girl means teaching her similar lessons, but also letting her know the world will sometimes give her a harder time. Respect will be harder to come by. You have to consider the little things, like the length of the skirts she wears. You have to try your damndest to give her a voice and release her out in the world knowing some might ignore it.

It's sort of a running joke with people that girls are notoriously difficult to raise. Every time I hear somebody say, "I have a daughter," you can guarantee some fuck donut is going to pipe up with "Ha! Good luck with that!" Oh, shut up, Charlie. *You're drunk*, Charlie.

Anyway, Charlie's not alone on the "good luck" front. Everybody's general reaction to "I have a daughter" is "good luck!" Is it because our society treats women like pretty little garbage cans or *beautiful little fools*, if you read *The Great Gatsby*? Sure! But also, no! If I prod Charlie a little more, perhaps by dangling a cocktail wiener over his head, he will probably burp out a couple of reasons why having and raising girls is such a burden. They *demand* things. You have to buy them a lot of stuff, like Barbies and day-of-the-week underwear. You have to teach them that when they get older, blood will pour out of them on a monthly basis. You have to beat away suitors with a stick. You worry about them constantly, because their reputation can be marred by outfit choice or sexual liberation. No doubt somebody will bring up the financial burden of one day having to finance their weddings. Not college, *weddings*. Cowabunga, dudes! I love all your attitudes!

When I was younger, I had twin dolls that I raised as my own plastic children. I named them "Baby Girl" and "Baby Boy." I know what you are thinking: "How did you come up with the name Baby Boy when the Beyoncé song of the same name didn't come out until 2003?" I never said I wasn't a visionary.

Anyway, Baby Boy was my *favorite*. I showered him with love and attention. He slept with me every night; I carried him lovingly in my arms everywhere I went and treated him like he was made of gold or the frosting in Dunkaroos. Baby Girl? I couldn't give less of a shit about her. I shoved her in the toy chest almost every night and tossed her around with the heft of an Olympic javelin thrower. Whenever my mom would inquire about her, I would say,

"I don't like her. She's too *difficult*."

I don't know where I learned it, but I certainly picked up on it: being a girl was the short end of the stick.

My mother loves to tell me she thought I was going to be a boy. This is interesting to me for a couple of reasons. First, if I *had been* a boy, she said she was going to name me Jonathan, which I think means I would have been a *sexy boy*. Secondly, the fact that she never chose to get the ultrasound that revealed my birth sex is absolutely bonkers to me.

My mother is a planner. She plans for Christmas in January. She plans menus and tablescapes and trips to Target. She makes numbered lists and bulleted lists and lists inside other lists. She is a woman of great preparation.

She is also a woman of little patience, a trait she graciously

bestowed on me. She and I, we don't want to wait fifteen minutes. We'd rather eat the toast only half-toasted and the eggs
half-cooked. I flip to the end of books when I can no longer
take the sexual tension of characters, just to see if one of them
dies or something. I check detailed movie reviews online to
decide if too many things "pop out" for me to want to see it. I
spend all day on GChat so I can receive every piece of gossip
from all my friends the second it happens. *I have to know everything, immediately.* I find it hard to believe she didn't want to
know what she was giving birth to. After all, this was my
mother, the lover of spoiler alerts, the one who can't even get
through an episode of *Game of Thrones* without conversations
like this:

"Alida, is he going to die?" (She's talking about Tyrion
Lannister, a man she has an enormously adorable crush on.)

"I'm not telling."

"Okay, well if you're not going to tell me, I'm not going to
watch it."

We flip to a movie that has a dog and Jennifer Aniston, or
something.

"Does the dog die? Because I'm not going to watch this if
the dog dies."

"I've never seen this."

"Okay, well, do you think the characters get together in the
end? Because I want them to get together in the end, and I
don't want to watch this if they don't."

Do you mean to tell me this impatient woman wasn't
about to find out the sex of her baby?

"I just had a feeling," she told me. "And I was eating a lot
of Big Macs."

Mom, I want to say. *The amount of hamburgers I can eat at any
given time is borderline macabre. This is not a decidedly male trait.*

So, there's no other real reason for her belief in a future Jonathan than her completely off-base intuition. Okay then. I asked my mother why she never got the ultrasound to see if she was right, and her answer was simply: "I wanted to be surprised."

I've come to the conclusion, then, that maybe ignorance was bliss. Maybe my parents wanted another boy. I wouldn't blame them if they did. It really is a hell of a cross to bear, to raise a girl. Baby boys don't come with as many warning labels. People talk about how rough and dirty boys get, but say it in a way that you know it builds character and is totally worth it. More a "handful" than a "headache." It's like they aren't even *worried* about their boys growing up. They say fun, happy stuff like "he's gonna carry on the family legacy" and "he's going to be a real lady killer one day," and they don't mean it in the "maybe one day they will kill women" way, though I suppose some of them do? That is a *joke*, by the way.

The day I was born, 99 percent female and 1 percent devil, my parents were through-the-roof ecstatic. I was adorable, I was alive, and they loved me more than they loved themselves. But having me meant new, uncharted territories. They had raised a son for three years. Gone was the quiet future of two sons who eventually went off to become investment bankers or baseball players or anything else that requires a starched uniform. Now they'd have to house and handle a female human—eighteen years through a twisted labyrinth of rising and falling emotions, periods and denim miniskirts, less pay and the giant worry that comes whenever she leaves the house.

My mother says the birth itself wasn't that bad. My brother's was a nightmare. He was a giant, sumo-wrestler baby. I was a peach pit, in comparison. For nine months, my mother had lugged me around in her stomach like a bowling ball that kicked her and demanded an endless supply of fast food. She said that I was small and difficult, and it still was the easiest I would ever be in the scheme of things.

I wonder, when I was born, when they finally brought me home from the hospital, if a question lingered on their minds:

"What now?"

I don't remember when I started learning how to be a girl, but I think it must have begun with toys.

When my brother was young, he played with monsters. Dinosaurs that shrieked when you pushed the buttons on their sides. Raptors whose flesh you could rip off. Werewolves, sharks, vampires, swords. G.I. Joes with utility belts full of guns. All kinds of things with sharp edges. I was intrigued, if not jealous.

Me? I don't think anybody specifically told me to *play house*, or how to play house, but I certainly got a dollhouse. My dollhouse was giant and pink, with blue shutters and about five bedrooms. All the different dolls I had in the dollhouse technically came with occupations on the box, which is progressive, except that I fucked it up majorly. My Barbie Doctor stayed home with the quintuplet Kellys I had amassed, and she wasn't even good at that gig, as they had no beds or real clothes. Ken usually just hung around, half-dressed, in another room, no job in sight. To say I was irresponsible was an understatement. If I was bored with Barbie and her hungry gaggle of children, I would take a break and play with the variety of kitchen-related toys at my disposal. I had a little Fisher-Price kitchen where I could fry up pretend hamburgers and eggs, as

well as an Easy Bake Oven where I could make something horrible and, unfortunately, edible, such as the Black Forest cake
that I believe gave my parents years of intestinal problems.

When my brother went off to school, I used to sneak into
his bedroom and take some of his toys. Army men would find
their way into my dollhouse bedrooms. Dinosaurs would become domesticated pets. Guns would become fashion accessories. My brother would wander into my bedroom when he got
home and eye me suspiciously. He knew I had taken some of
his toys, as they would come back wearing aprons or tiny
Pocahontas necklaces.

Eventually, our parents just gave us one big playroom
where we dumped all this crap and could fight our doll-related
custody battles on our own turf. There, we had army battles in
cookie ovens and watched giant spiders invade baby bedrooms. The Terminator married Teresa, the Sega Genesis eventually ruled all, and we forgot the idea of gendered toys in that
giant carpeted room. This pile of crap taught me something
about myself—what I *liked*, what I *enjoyed*, not just the sparkly
shit they marketed to girls. As it stood, I *was* pretty delicate and
feminine, and also liked to create a household filled with monsters that would eat the heads of my little Polly Pockets and
Quints. Yet, when I went to school, all I could do was play with
the Pretty Princesses and the dolls. The boys would sit over on
the other side of the classroom with all the monsters. I lost half
my world and all my dinosaurs. There, I was stuck cooking for
a series of ungrateful dolls, waiting for my Prince Charming, a
T. rex who would eat all their heads, to make his way over to
the girls' side of the classroom. He never came.

*   *   *

When I first moved to Brooklyn, I lived across from a middle school. One day, my friend Ian and I were taking a walk as kids were getting let out of school for the day.

"You know," I say, "I've considered slapping on a backpack and pretending to be a student for a week. Kind of like Josie Grossie in *Never Been Kissed* but without the completely unethical teacher-student relationship as the crux of the story."

Ian thinks. "I'd see if I could get in there and pretend to be an inspirational teacher à la *Dead Poets Society*. And the first thing I'd do is throw a chair across the room and scream, *Gender is a construct!!!*"

I think this story is really funny, but the more I think about it, the more I think it's not the worst idea. I'm sure he would get arrested because it's also an *illegal idea*, but I wish this *were* the kind of thing kids learned early on. Gender doesn't determine the things you like, your hobbies, or your personality. I didn't squeeze out of my mother grabbing at tiny bracelets and high heels. My brother didn't have a strand of DNA that meant he loved monster trucks. This is the kind of stuff we pick up when we start getting different Happy Meal toys. In fact, the idea that little boys and little girls are different from each other is mostly on us. It stems from parents' fears that they will have some sort of societally weird child, which most of us end up being in high school anyway. Having your baby daughters only play with dolls won't stop a hearty Goth phase from happening! It won't stop your kid from being gay! It won't do anything but plant the idea that girls are good for kitchen stuff and boys who play with dolls are "pussies." It won't do *anything* but harm.

So yes, the second a baby pops out of the oven, we start establishing the massive differences between boys and girls, in a time where they are all throwing up on themselves and are pretty much in the same league. The first way we do this is with clothes. I am aware that we need to *decorate babies* because all babies look like screaming raisins, and you cannot tell them apart to save your own life. When I was born, I looked like an animatronic Disney World animal. With eyes the size of tiny saucers and tufts of brown hair that stuck straight out of my head like crabgrass, I was Animal Kingdom's newest lemur. Very "cute." Father's nose and mother's eyes. And my family immediately wanted to amplify that cuteness. You can't just slap a baby in a white onesie and call it a day—you gotta jazz that shit up! Once my aunts and uncles had their way with me, I looked like a lemur on her way to her first *quinceañera*. In photos, my head would be weighed down with sunflower hats, my jackets bedazzled to be seen from satellites close to the Earth's orbit. Everything about me screamed Girl, or at least *"Golden Girl!"* I wore enough hot pink to outfit at least thirty walkathons and four hundred bachelorette parties.

My brother, three years my senior and, at the time, still considered a baby by society's standards, escaped much of this extreme decorating during childhood. In terms of costume attire, there are two photos of my brother: one of him as a Ghostbuster and one of him as a cop. Otherwise he wore Alf T-shirts and the inoffensive Baby Gap polo. In many pictures of us, he looks like he's interrupting an Anne Geddes photo shoot where the theme was maybe "Liza Minnelli."

In case the garish attire didn't throw off enough signals, people took to reminding my parents just how much of a girl I was. My dad was the biggest target of these comments.

"You better start polishing that shotgun, Bill. You're going to have to beat those fellows off at the door," a cousin casually sounded off, as if the world were about to breed the undead right at my doorstep.

"You know, one day the boys are going to be chasing her

down the block!" he heard on more than one occasion. Ah, yes, nothing like a subtle assault reference said about a baby who's still pooping on herself. It's so fun to have a girl!

"You remember what it's like to be young!" they would say. By all accounts, my dad had had little to no experience "being young" in the way they were referencing. My father never ran around chasing women down the block. He was a brilliant guy, who spent much of his early years designing blueprints and reading books. There was no chasing, lest his nerdy glasses would fall off and break.

Each of these warnings foretold a bleak future for my dad: one day his little princess was going to get breasts and get chased around like an animal. To prepare for this, he unintentionally created what I can only refer to as a garage that Leatherface would be proud of.

My father has always been big on building stuff. He has always managed to fix any appliance that was broken. He has a tractor that is so old it doesn't look like a real tractor anymore; it looks like something you would see in a really boring museum. The fact that I had never seen a plumber or a mechanic until I moved into my own apartment should paint the picture that there were plenty of tools in his garage. As a kid, I was quite talented at dodging past the wall of axes, the hanging chainsaw, the giant tractors, the motorcycles, and the hundreds of wrenches just to tell him lunch was ready. And it wasn't just the tools that gave the garage an eerie feel. There was the deer skull my father found in the backyard and bleached to preserve, baby sharks and a baby bat in jars, and just to add to the menagerie, a taxidermied pheasant. If any fifteen-year-old boy didn't enter the garage and think he was going to end up disembodied in a freezer somewhere, he was most likely Norman Bates himself.

Not that my dad would ever feel the need to intimidate a potential date. My dad is one of the most forward-thinking people I've ever met who also rides an old tractor. He is a feminist by my definition rather than his—because the moment he had a daughter, I believe he became one, on account of how damned hard he tried to give me all the advantages my brother had. He did his best to prepare me for the years ahead.

Sometimes, he tried to instill in me just how scary the world could be. He would sit me at the table and tell me the tales of Abercrombie and Fitch, a detective pair he invented who would solve gruesome murders. I wasn't allowed to leave the table until I figured out that the missing weapon was an ICICLE!!!! Icicles, by the way, are the only murder weapon that can *dissolve*. My dad would describe in detail the plot of *The War of the Worlds*. "What would YOU do if aliens came down and began to destroy the world at large?" Answer: run, hope for the best, carry a water bottle. We would watch daylong marathons of *The Twilight Zone*, until I became acutely aware that dolls, other humans, beings from another planet, and William Shatner brought fear and danger into the world.

Sometimes, my dad would talk to me about reaching my potential. He would teach me about world history, or sit with me while I did my math homework, no matter how much I insisted that I would never understand it. He taught me how to win battles, and theories about the universe, and told me about lots of science-y smart things I thought I would never be interested in. And, ever the *Star Trek* fan, he also instilled in me the one goal I should strive for in adulthood: Live Long and Prosper.

And when he wasn't teaching me about how terrifying and wonderful the world was, my father would do my hair.

Once I reached about six years old, I had this unforgiving mane of curly brown hair that, to be honest, would do best in a cartoon about a precocious girl detective. Whenever I got out of the shower, it would become a dripping wet mess of Medusa knots that not even No More Tears conditioner could calm down. It needed more attention, and that's where my dad would come in.

Every day, I would waddle up to my parents' bathroom and stare up at my father until he agreed to do my hair. He sat me on the dresser and would ask me the same question:

"Alida, do you want to be a princess or a troll?"

On some days, I wanted to be beautiful. He would then blow-dry my hair in a normal fashion and off I would go to school. But some days? Some days, I would want to run wild. To not be beautiful. To be the chaser, rather than the chased. And on those days, he would flip my head over and make a mess of things. I would trot away with the look of a girl who had just been electrocuted, and I would be happy.

It was one of the most important lessons of my childhood. Whether or not he did it on purpose: the garage of weapons, the tales of crime, the belief that you did not always have to be beautiful, I've never asked. All I know is that at eleven a.m. on August 23, 1988, my father realized he would have to raise a girl. He knew what would come with it: the headaches, the worry, and the hope she would turn out okay. He taught me all the things he could: how to think critically, how to listen, how not to be bored by history, what kinds of cheese go best with crackers. He taught me how to question things, to be smart, and sassy, and sarcastic, and how to never believe everything that you hear. He taught my brother similar things, in a world where the toys made for my brother were about dreaming and the toys made for me were about keeping me chained to the ground.

Either way, he did what he could, and still he knew one

thing: despite all this, he never knew if I would be okay, or be safe. He didn't know if I would get the same educational opportunities, or if people would love me for my brain, or like my smile, or listen to me when I spoke.

Maybe that's what's really scary when the doctor tells you it's a girl.

For the record, I hope that when I have children (I do want to have children), I have at least one girl.

I want the opportunity to raise a warrior child. A girl with self-esteem, a girl who learns about saying no, and a girl who learns how to be herself in a world that doesn't always want her to. I think the next generation of girls is going to have a coat of arms: a giant, cocked eyebrow and the word "NO." Maybe some dark lipstick thrown in there for good measure. I've seen girls grow up into women, and I want to be a part of it.

Wish me luck, Charlie. Wish me luck, Dad.

Mutt

There was an infamous argument that happened between my parents when I was young, and it was about my ears.

It started when my mother mentioned to my dad, casually, that it was almost time to pierce their daughter's ears.

My mom had a real fondness for accessorizing her child—she loved adding bows, headbands, baseball caps, bonnets, on and around my head. So, of course, it was no surprise that jewelry entered the mix when I was just under a year old. "Come on! Let's make her look even busier!"

My father's response was apparently something along the lines of: "... *what?!*" He waited for a laugh track, a nudge, some kind of sign that my mother was joking. It was enough that I wore tiny bracelets. Do you know how hard it is to close a tiny bracelet on a *baby*?

Of course, my mother was not kidding. My mother's ears were pierced when she was just a baby. My grandmother numbed the area with ice, rubbed it down with alcohol, and sterilized one of her sewing needles. Barely a second later, the tiny gold studs went in and that was that. My mother doesn't remember any of it, she argued. It was also *very sterile* and *perfectly safe*.

Thirty years later, my grandmother still had a steady hand and a desire to shove a pair of peridot studs into her first and only granddaughter's ears. "Her *birthstone*," she added, as if this piece of information worked in her favor. She also had a pair of diamond crosses if the birthstones were too New Agey. She bought all this as soon as her daughter gave birth to a daughter, because she had been piercing the women in her family for a long time, as is the tradition with Puerto Rican women. They start wearing tiny gold hoops, followed by iced mocha nail polish soon after that. If you are Puerto Rican, I guarantee your mother has some sort of Revlon Iced Mocha nail polish from 1989 with a Caldor sticker still on it. That's just how it is.

My mother hadn't prepared for my father's resistance. She had barely even flinched during the piercing itself! She had only turned very, very red and screamed afterward, but my grandmother claims this was because of how cold the ice was. Babies do not like ice, although apparently they are okay with sharp objects. This was my mother's argument, hanging on by a thread.

My father's response: "No."

Not surprisingly, it was the image of my mother as a baby, tomato-red and screaming, that sealed the deal. To say I was a daddy's girl was an understatement. He had already named me His Little Peanut. He was not about to put a needle near or into The Peanut unless it prevented polio.

"But look how even my ears are! It's like it was done by a professional." (Let the record show that my grandmother did in fact do an excellent job.)

My father: "*No*." His anti-ear-piercing wasn't just no, it was "We'll let her decide when she wants to get her ears pierced." And that was that.

My mother had lost this round, but she wasn't offended. During their many years of marriage, my parents have clashed over enough cultural differences to fill an immigrant boat or a sitcom. You win some, you lose some. You learn to adjust. You have mayo in your house, which my mom never tried until she was eighteen, and you have *morcilla*,* the ingredients of which she kept from my father for most of his life. You listen to Linda Ronstadt and you listen to Tito Puente and you listen to the Rolling Stones.

If you are their *daughter*, you wear outrageously elaborate Puerto Rican dresses, sent by your grandfather, that make Christmas photos look as if you were raised by Liberace. If you are their *daughter*, this prompts the other side of your family to buy you knitted hats with the Irish flag on them, which make other Christmas photos look like you were raised by a band of craft-happy leprechauns.

Christmas, or deleted scene from
Behind the Candelabra?

---

* Dad, *morcilla* is made from pig's blood, by the way. You've been eating pig's blood. Haven't you ever heard of black pudding? Are you not really Irish?

Like I said, you learn to adjust.

If I were old enough to have a horse (or even hold up my head without support) in the ear-piercing race, I would have interjected with a sentence I have thought or said, over and over, during the course of my whole life.

"Dad. You just don't *understand*."

In some households, that phrase is uttered when parents are being technologically inept (like by signing their names on Facebook wall posts), or because they aren't letting you go to a party, or if they don't like your outfit choices. In my house, it meant that my dad was either not understanding my feminine mystique or he was being very *white*. My dad, bless his wonderful heart, is *very white*. He reads the *Wall Street Journal* and dances only with his arms. He can walk past any police officer in the world without arousing suspicion. He feels that children should be somewhat responsible for their own decisions. I can tell you that this kind of freedom of choice is *a white thing*. The idea that children should do things *when they want to* is the kind of white parenting idea that ranks right up there with "you need to take a time-out," and "what would *you* like for dinner?" My mother got sick *one time* and my dad made me and my brother dinner. We got to pick whatever we wanted. "Wagon Wheels!" We screamed for the pasta. We requested no vegetables.

And we got it.

But being biracial wasn't just comically opposing values. It wasn't just a television sitcom where the dad shakes his head while the mother talks about salsa dancing or tries to get him to say words in Spanish. It was confusing. It felt different. I knew other people's parents, and they weren't like mine—as in the children *looked like* their parents. I didn't look like mine. My olive-y pale skin, my brown hair, my fat nose and curves and squat shortness didn't come from either. It was just a mix.

The best way to demonstrate this hybridity is to observe the Nugent family in the summertime. There isn't a bottle of sunscreen large enough or SPF high enough to save my father from sunburn. He has to wear baseball hats and T-shirts to the beach, or else he would turn so red people would draw butter and try to crack his claws off. On the other hand, I can never recall a time my mother needed more than a drop of sunscreen. Her skin was already the kind of tan that white people would *pay for.* When you put me out in the hot sun for an hour, however, my skin turns into a Baskin-Robbins caramel sundae. I'm all dark brown skin and a bright red cherry that becomes my gringo nose and my gringo shoulders. A perfect combo, or an imperfect combo, depending on when you asked me about it in life.

For a long time, I didn't like calling myself biracial. I was "Puerto Rican" all the time, or Irish on Saint Patrick's Day, or a "Heinz 57," which was my dad's phrase for dogs that were mutts. I liked "mutt." The word "biracial" always felt alienating. It was "Well, which do you look like more? Which one are you more of?"

The way I always saw it, I was Puerto Rican living in a middle-class white suburb for most of my life. I felt this made me "mostly white" to everybody *but* white people. To other Puerto Ricans or minorities, I was living a white life with organic hamburger restaurants and North Faces and *Everybody Loves Raymond.* I had the privilege that came with the kind of curly hair that didn't kink up like my mother's. I had the privilege of finding foundation colors in the drugstore that matched my skin. I had the privilege of feeling safe, of hiding in the racially ambiguous look that doesn't get you followed around stores by security.

To my white friends, I was the diversity badge. I was the

Puerto Rican friend. I was the "so what do you eat for dinner?!" friend and the "it's so unfair you're going to get into
better colleges than I do because you get to say you're Latina!"
friend. *I don't know, man. It's not like I'm ALL Latina. It's not like
I'm not white, too.*

This made me feel guilty, or like a liar. Being biracial always felt like I was standing on a rooftop, watching both sides
of the street. I could see them both, but I never really felt like I
deserved to be on the sidewalk. I wasn't sure where my experience fit in on the spectrum. Being a white woman is not the
same as being a Hispanic woman, just like being African-
American isn't the same as being Hispanic, or Asian. All are
different experiences, with different privileges and different
difficulties. Each culture faces challenges that are unique. Each
needs different spaces, different conversations, and different
acknowledgments. I felt uncomfortable by the implications of
these differences for a very long time—I didn't want to choose.
So, instead, I described myself as a mutt. I was the mix of
things you couldn't place. Nobody ever thought I was white.
Nobody ever thought I was Latina, or part Doberman, or even
German shepherd.

But I mean, people *loved* to guess. Olive-toned people are
walking guessing games, and the game is called "So, what *are*
you???" My best friend in high school, whose mother was
African-American, got the opposite. Her game was "so . . . are
you . . . like . . . *100 percent* black???" Either way, racially ambiguous kids spend much of their time correcting people on
their ethnicities.

I've been Iranian a lot. I've been Greek sometimes. I've
been Italian, Armenian, Egyptian, and . . . "I can't place it! *I just
can't place it!*" People will stare at me, squinting. They want to
ask, "Do you say Parmesan like Parm-ee-john-o?? Do you roll

your *r*'s? Do you want *kafta*? *Mortadella*? *Tzatziki*? *Pollo*?!" I count down silently in my head until they finally say something. They are trying to decide how to phrase it. They are trying to decide if they should say something like "so . . . where are you from?" I would reply that I was born in a hospital in Mount Kisco, New York. They are trying to decide if it's polite to guess. They are trying to decide if they should just list different ethnicities and see what makes my ears perk up.

"You must be . . . Israeli. You *have* to be." This came from the woman I'd served coffee to almost a thousand times. I knew her long game. She had asked me, weeks before, "how I got my unique name." I was named after Alida Valli, an Italian actress who starred in a movie called *The Third Man*. Her eyes lit up.

"I'm not Italian." Her eyebrows furrowed into the back of her skull. She said something about my strong eyebrows (which I know is also code for: you have hairy arms) and walked away.

"Well are you Greek or something?!" This was her, a couple of days later. I hand her her coffee. I say I am Puerto Rican and Irish, and maybe a bit German.

"So, Spanish?"

"No. Puerto Rican. And Irish." Spanish means you're European, and many Europeans would be *very offended* if I identified as Spanish. I've got that dirty blood. I'm Latina. It's *so different*, but only to Hispanic people.

She looked at me. "What a weird combo! I don't see it."

Sure, lady. When I look in the mirror, I don't really see it either.

I know I'm biracial because, sometimes, things are split up. I bring home bagels and plantains for my parents when I go to visit them. I know I'm biracial because half my family tells me I look good when the other half tells me "you too skinny" and tries to force food down my throat. I know I'm biracial because when I was a kid, watching the New Year's Eve countdown meant switching between composed newscasters making small talk in bright dresses and the champagne drunk fest that is the Univision broadcast. My skin is oily at the forehead and dry at the cheeks. I can roll my *r*'s and eat mashed potatoes by the gallon and I can merengue but I watch people Riverdance. I have tall, blond, Southern cousins and a great-uncle-cousin-very-removed who practices Santeria.

Believe me. I know what I'm made of. I'm just not 100 percent sure who I *am*, and how it defines me, and if it's easier to just split myself in half and hope for the best.

This was an issue when I became a feminist. When you become a feminist, you become very aware of the importance of "claiming" an identity. "Feminist" was really the first label I claimed that I was comfortable with, and it felt good.

I was always loose with labels. The only previous experience I had with them was from the men I was sleeping with, who would tell me in a cigarette-and-whiskey-soaked voice: "Babe, I don't believe in labels. Why do we have to even define what we are?" And it meant, really, that a man didn't want to be sleeping with me for much longer. "No labels" is pretty easy for straight white boys to say. It's pretty easy for people who are the "majority" of anything to say. As a straight person, I never had to think deeply about how I could present myself to the world. As a cis female, I never had to search the catacombs of the Internet in order to find somebody who identified as me; I could just walk down the street. Most of my labels were handed to me upon birth. I was lucky that some of the labels handed to me were ones I was comfortable with. That is not always the case. When I became a feminist, I realized how sometimes, *choosing* a label you feel strongly aligned with can be freeing. It's empowering to find the word that you can identify with, that *says* something about you, and it's empowering to be able to claim it. However, to lead an authentic life, you can't just *choose* labels you feel make your life easier, just to comfortably identify with something that people can digest. This is where my own labels get problematic.

For a long time, I thought biracial was an identity that was too complicated to chew on. I didn't really love being white. White people were problematic. They had a history of taking things (usually from the ancestry that makes up my other half), and I just didn't dig it.

I had always, always liked being Latina more than anything else. Instead of saying I was biracial, and sometimes instead of just saying "mutt," I would say that I was Puerto Rican. I enjoyed being Latina because the women of my family, specifically my mother and my grandmother, told me so much about being a *Puerto Rican Woman*—stories of growing up in Puerto Rico and eating coconut ice and playing in the ocean to find crabs. It spoke to my soul. It made me feel like I had a history, deep in my blood. This still resonates with me. I see pictures of Puerto Rico, a place I visited often in my childhood, and I yearn for it. The first time I visited San Juan, my mother grabbed my hand as the plane descended and whispered, *"Tu isla."* I remember it because it struck me in my heart. When people find a home, it sticks with them.

But it took me much, much longer to realize that finding a home is not the end of it.

I had to understand that I was both Latina and white. To deny another part of myself was denying the privileges, hardships, and experiences that came with my heritage. To not identify with white is offensive to the side of me that is Latina, to not recognize the privileges that come with being a *white person*. And to not identify as white is to deny my history. It was important to be both, but I just didn't know *how* to be both. Not only did I feel unfit for the job, I never really wanted it in the first place.

The first time I was called a spic, I was in fifth grade.

My family had just moved from a more racially diverse neighborhood to a tiny suburb in Westchester County. South Salem was a *very* white town. It had trees and little mailboxes that looked like houses, in front of real houses. There was a festival every September that celebrated *honey* or maybe *apple cider* or maybe *farms.* My parents said the public schools were better. I used to live real close to a Taco Bell, and a Kmart. Now, I lived within walking distance of the rich part of Connecticut, in a town that unfurled an American flag the size of a building nearly every holiday the post office was closed. It's *that kind of town.*

My mother had been moving away from racially diverse neighborhoods ever since she married my father. She grew up in Washington Heights, New York. This was a real Puerto Rican hood. This was why, I'm serious, she had never eaten mayonnaise before she started dating my dad. My dad grew up in the Bronx. He was skinny and handsome in the way that Blake from *Workaholics* is handsome, because he looked like Blake from *Workaholics.* He used to play basketball in the parking lot of the church my mother attended, which is kind of like buying your groceries in a town that is forty-five minutes away. That might sound nuts unless you are me, who takes the subway to Queens just to eat a dumpling. Anyway, during one of those basketball games, he spotted my mom. He thought she was gorgeous, because she was. I have to put out a disclaimer right now that this is a true story and not just me describing the plot of *Love and Basketball,* but yes, they started dating.

Part of their relationship was very centered around how bad my mother's neighborhood was for white boys. It was bad for white boys because everybody knew why they were there. White boys in that hood meant they were there to take pretty little mamas on dates. Interracial dating was a *weird* thing at that time. Some people were very *West Side Story*, "I want to kill you both" about it. Others were very "Please, date the white man and have him buy you good shoes and jewelry" about it. My mother's family was just, "Oh, please don't date one of those awful hippies," which is a parenting tip that has been passed on to me, too.

But my dad wasn't deterred. He kept showing up, becoming known in the neighborhood as Rainbow Man because of the bright sweaters he wore. He used to ride his motorcycle to meet my mom, which, *believe me*, is funny because he used to put three hundred layers on me when I started to learn how to ride a tricycle. He had to eventually park this motorcycle in the hallway of my mother's apartment, on account of how many times the radio was stolen. Despite this, my grandmother did not want him to enter the house because he had this long golden hair, which meant *hippie and you know the deal.*

But one day, the fridge in my grandmother's apartment was broken. My dad was not really a hippie, despite his appearance. He was more of a handyman, and so he fixed the fridge. You know that food is the way to any normal human being's heart, right? So it worked.

A couple of years later, my parents graduated college and got married. My mom wanted to move to Queens and live in a brownstone. My father wanted to move out of the city, altogether, to live a quieter life.

My mother said this was an *adjustment*. She had to learn how to drive a car. She had to explain to stock boys that plantains weren't just unripe bananas. She had to deal with people who wore tiny little lobsters on their shirts and pants. Sometimes, when she drives me to the Metro-North station so I can take the train back to New York City, that gaping Iron Monster she once called home, I think she misses it. She often tells me about stores that have closed, like the five and dime, or about how people used to use tokens instead of MetroCards in the subway, and I can tell that her heart is still there, in a way. I tell her she's not missing much, as literally nothing in New York City costs either five or a dime anymore.

Life may have been different than she originally imagined, but she also loves the change that came with leaving the city. She has a house that she gets to fit an offensive amount of Christmas trees in, trees she loads with all the crap ornaments I made in elementary school, and about forty-six devoted to different dogs we owned. And those dogs we had got to run around our own backyard, and eat deer poo in our own backyard, and chew up my dad's slippers there, too. My mother has a washer and a dryer and a big fridge. It was heaven all topped off with schools that were free and actually pretty good.

"The biggest change about moving from the city," my mother told me, "was how people talked about me and your father. They always asked me how I *dealt* with being in an interracial relationship. Honestly, I had never thought I was *dealing* with it at all!" She didn't really have to think about it before because my father, white in his rainbow sweaters, was the outsider. When she moved to a neighborhood where most people are white, *she* became the outsider.

"Oh. And most people think I'm a nanny."

I knew nothing about these kinds of adjustments. I moved from one suburban house to another, a little caffè-latte-colored kid who knew nothing about the struggle. I'm quite sure this was my parents' intention. But when I was ten, I was called a spic by a kid named Brian. *Brian*, who used to chew on his *own sleeves in class*. I'm not sure if this was part of the American Dream for my parents, having kids that got called racial slurs by the dumbest kids in the class, but here I was. I'll never forget the scene: I was tending the class garden, probably learning lessons about sustainable farming I've never picked up on. The teacher said that we had to make sure to get the dirt off our hands, that we had to be spic-and-span by the time we had left. Brian turned to me.

"Spic. Like you."

There wasn't a person around us when he said it, so he didn't say it to shock anyone, or seem cool. It was almost like he was testing the waters of being cruel to someone. I remember his face: a little half-smirk, half-scared look. He was learning how it felt to say things that hurt people, and I couldn't even tell if he liked it. I knew what the word meant, because when you're ethnic you learn those words real early on to prepare your armor when they are directed at you. But still, hearing it directed toward me, it stopped me dead in my tracks.

Before this happened, I used to talk a lot about how I wasn't white. Being the newish kid in a nice neighborhood, this was a "cool factoid" about me that separated me from the others, like the kid who had crutches or was adopted. I would say I was Hispanic because it made me memorable to other people. I was proud and excited to reveal it. It took me a while to realize that being ethnic wasn't always *cool*.

The cruelest kind of words cut you for the things you can't change: your race, your ethnicity, your sexuality. People use these words because it makes them feel superior to you, because they were taught that having a different race, a different ethnicity, or a different sexuality is *bad*. People use them because they think others are less than they are, because this country was built on the idea that white men are superior to everybody else, and because it was built on the backs of those who did not fit that ideal. It's ugly, but man, it's true. People use these words because there is no defense to them. I couldn't say, "Hey! That's not me!" How could I retort? So instead, I just learned. I learned that sometimes people would get at you for the things you couldn't change, *just because you couldn't change them*. I learned people would use their words to cut me down. So, when somebody called me a cunt for the first time, I was almost *ready* for it. I knew how people loved to say things they knew could really sting (for the record: it was at a Boston University keg party, and he called me a cunt because I drunkenly cut in front of him on line to get beer. Very, very, VERY warranted!). And I prepared myself for it.

Brian wouldn't be the last person who called me a spic or a wetback. I was called stupid, hurtful names by ignorant people a couple more times when I was growing up. The truth is, however, I grew up in the kind of polite town that didn't use nasty words. You learn how people really feel, I think, through actions.

I learned how people really felt when they were uncomfortable with me. When my friend Rosa, who was from Spain, told her mother I was Puerto Rican and not Spanish, her mother's warm attitude toward me shifted. You can feel it when people don't like who you are; they have an icy formality and an air that they are doing me a favor just by letting me stand near them. When I mention to some people that I'm Puerto Rican and they didn't know before, every once in a while you can see a flicker in their eyes, a distaste, an "oh God, have I been drunk enough in front of this chick to let it slip how I really feel?" Although, to be honest, 99 percent of the time I can take a shot in the dark and *guess* who uses phrases like "those people." Call it a sixth sense, or an "I've seen the kinds of articles you post on Facebook" sense.

I also learned how people really felt when they were *comfortable* with me. Man, when people get really comfortable with you, they tell you all kinds of stuff you wish you didn't know. They make jokes about how your mom must clean houses, or how I eat Goya beans out of cans (I actually DO do this), or how I probably am good at mowing lawns (I am not skilled at moving machinery, sorry). They ask if all my family is legal. Just a lot of different things people should probably not say:

"I've always wanted to be with a Latina girl. I actually find them super attractive." Great! So do I! You don't win points for finding another race attractive!

"Well, you probably got into Emerson because . . . you have some advantages I don't." This always drove me crazy. *Yo*, I got into Emerson because I was willing to put myself into debt for the opportunity to not have to take math classes. I am not the picture of affirmative action you are looking for.

And the classic homage to Karen-from-*Mean-Girls* comment:

"If you're Latina . . . why don't you have an *ass*?"

Here are my responses to that: (a) I don't know why I have a flat ass. I would love to have a big ass because my breasts have always been huge and the odd proportions make buying dresses super difficult. (b) Oh, now that the big booty is a fashion trend, everybody loves a fat ass? I distinctly remember everybody wanting flat asses, just like I distinctly remember hoop earrings and baby hairs and cornrows being out until high fashion and Miley Cyrus and Katy Perry got a hold of 'em. But, you know, keep telling Nicki Minaj her ass in a thong is graphic, and keep putting Iggy Azalea in songs like "Booty."

(c) This kind of thing is called erasure, and it happens a lot to people who can go from feeling invisible to being targeted at nearly any turn. And finally (d) I actually like spicy food so do I get to have my Latina card now?

People, whether or not I'm comfortable with them, still tell me they find me *exotic*. Do not describe people as exotic, please. It's the kind of thing people say to ethnic women, animals in the zoo, and spicy cuisine. Now, here's something that I have to mention about all this. *I easily, easily present as a white person.* Ethnically ambiguous, like I've mentioned, but not many look at me and think, *That's a Latina*.

And while I learned at a young age that being Hispanic was complicated, I learned something else as I got older: when I went to a job interview, *I could be white, and I could get a job, and probably a better-paying job.* When studies mention that women make seventy-seven cents for every dollar a man makes, there's a distinction that's often forgotten: that's the statistic for *white women*. African-American women make sixty-two cents for every dollar. Hispanic women make fifty-four cents for every dollar.

So I also had to learn that I didn't have it the worst by a long shot. I had to learn that it was worse for others, and if you are white or white-passing you have to learn that, too. I can hide. I had to learn that my mother's dark skin, my grandmother's dark skin, made it harder for them. You have to learn that people with dark skin are treated differently, that there are assumptions made about them immediately. You have to learn that happens everywhere, every day. That's why I call myself biracial, and why I call myself a feminist. Mainstream feminism sometimes forgets these different experiences. I cannot. I know because I've been called a bitch and I've been called a spic. We have to examine the different stories, the different issues, and the different struggles that every woman has. We cannot let just white women lead the way. We have to speak, in all our different voices, to tell our unique stories. I will always tell mine.

Being biracial means I'm lucky enough to see the rich and different histories of my family, and see where and how those made me: My grandmother left my grandfather to move to New York City and raise her daughter as a single mother. My grandmother on my father's side raised four children in the Bronx, all of whom went to college. My parents grew up to be two people in a house in the suburbs who like to stay home and watch Food Network together, and celebrate their dog's birthdays. I sometimes eat delicious and homemade rice and beans, but mostly I just hear about my parents' obsession with any show that has Guy Fieri.

Still, I have complicated blood in my veins. In the summer, you see the sunburn on my shoulders, the deep tan on my face and chest, and you might be able to guess where I came from.

"Oh, I'm biracial," I say. "Puerto Rican, and Irish, too." I am both.

My identity comes from how I feel. My identity is the feeling and memory of Puerto Rico when it is so humid and hot out that my hair finds new ways to rebel. It is walking through the streets of Old San Juan and discovering that chicken soup in Puerto Rico often comes with the feet sticking right out of it. It is the giant tree that my grandfather chopped down himself when he hurt his foot picking the fruit from it because he gets as mad at inanimate objects as I do. It is convincing my mom to buy me piña coladas when I was seventeen. It is drinking beer on Saint Patrick's Day with my brother; it is the Irish crest with two gold lions on a black background (I'd be a Lannister, for sure); it is the sound of bagpipes and the taste of beef stew I can only eat three bites of. It is all of it.

My identity is how I look: my curly hair and lighter skin and big brown eyes. It is the traits I get from my mother and the traits I get from my dad. It is seeing myself in other women and seeing myself in the mirror. My identity as a woman of two different ethnicities is the acknowledgment of the privileges I have, and the privileges I won't ever have, and the privileges and problems that the women in that group have to deal with. It is a reminder of how lucky I am, and how other women aren't as fortunate. My identity is mine to claim, good and bad, just like yours. To understand it, and understand what it means in the state of the world, and what it means to others, is a priceless lesson for a feminist, or a woman, or a human being.

I still keep an old pair of peridot studs in a jewelry box at my parents' house. If I ever have a daughter, I'm not sure what I'll do with them. I just know I will tell her about my grandmother, and my dad, and me, and all the swirling histories of her past, and she will begin to learn it all.

Girl Under Control

Cross-legged on the couch, I am thinking about the complexities of life, and how quickly everything can change. I am thinking about the last time I had my period, and why I never keep track of it. I am thinking about a third bowl of cereal, and mostly, I am delaying taking the damn pregnancy test that is staring me in the face.

Yes, in these moments of reckoning, I am procrastinating. I usually procrastinate on insignificant stuff like e-mail and laundry, so, naturally, I am putting all my effort into facing this potentially life-altering moment. I managed to avoid buying the test for a week, until I could no longer handle my anxiety and headed to Duane Reade, and then, because my procrastination knows no bounds, the supermarket. I stock up on very necessary items such as Reese's Puffs, American cheese, and frozen yogurt. Without a doubt if there was ever a disaster in New York City, I would die, because these are my crisis essentials. After wandering my neighborhood hoping to suddenly feel any sign of a menstrual cramp, I retreated back home, crashed on my futon, turned on *The Real Housewives*, and avoided sipping water at all costs.

This wasn't how it was supposed to go that day. I was supposed to take the test, and after that I was supposed to go for a run to clear my head, then eat a delightful egg-white frittata, and do other responsible things like organizing my receipts or starting a capsule wardrobe. But I am the Queen of Avoidance. I would much rather eat sugar and avoid the world than face this terrifying situation. I was twenty-four and I was mad at myself because I couldn't be grown-up, or responsible, or face things like pregnancy.

The only other time I had ever seen a pregnancy test was in high school, when I worked at Starbucks. Girls would go to the Starbucks bathrooms and take tests there so their parents would never find out. I found the tests, though. I had to clean them off the floor, in a hearty mixture of "really? The floor?" and "well, *cleaning* pregnancy tests in high school isn't as rock bottom as *taking them*, I suppose." Silver lining!

But now I was that girl who needed to take one. I didn't feel twenty-four, an age when having a child isn't even that ridiculous. Twenty-four years old, an age when some women are raising families and not living in apartments that are decorated with old vodka bottles. I thought about how I wasn't ready to be a mother. I thought about how I had just moved to New York and still had college loans and couldn't even keep a plant alive. I could kill a plant just by looking at it, weeks after I had forgotten to water it. I felt stupid, and I felt helpless. Because *that* is how you feel when you are about to take a pregnancy test you don't want to take. It doesn't feel like it's just you and your decision—it feels like it's you and your failure to be a functioning human being. Instead of excitement, or reflection, it is a moment of shame.

Finally, I muster up the courage to take it. It lies inanimate on my bathroom sink, and I am staring at it with a lot of hatred.

I hate that you have to put it "pointed flat but not downward" as it says in the instructions. Why would I point it downward when it's covered in my pee? What is *pointed flat*? Mostly, I hate it because my future is held in its dopey plastic.

The minutes that pass don't feel like minutes. They are hours covered in molasses, strapped on to the back of a turtle or any old lady. They are "waiting for a subway when you have to pee" minutes. They are the "three minutes before work ends on Friday" minutes. They are "waiting for your food to come when you haven't eaten all day" minutes. They are slooooooooow.

To pass the time, I recall how embarrassing it was to buy the pregnancy test in the first place. I didn't go right to the aisle where I knew they were sold, the one right by the pharmacy counter where I have spent time staring at different condom boxes when waiting to refill a prescription. Instead, I went to the makeup aisle and spent a few minutes contemplating if pregnant women looked good in dramatic cat eye (of course they do), then to the shampoo aisle to see if there was something I could add to my hair to achieve volume for around five minutes before it inevitably goes limp. Finally, I grabbed a couple of hair ties and paper towels and probably a bottle of diet soda because you *do not simply walk into a drugstore and buy a pregnancy test without other products you can add to the basket to cover it.*

In a way, I am used to it. I am used to the odd shameful feeling that comes with buying in a drugstore products that mostly have to do with being a woman. Let's rank from least to most embarrassing the feminine products you can purchase at your local Duane Reade. Tampons kick off the list. They are ace. Everybody knows what you can do while wearing tampons: practically everything. Dance. Wear silky white pajamas.

Go on horseback, even in the water. In the years that we've been perfecting the mechanics of a woman's period, the tampon has become queen. Even the girls in the commercials are cool now. They wear leather jackets and hoodies and speak to me like they understand me. "I get you, cool cat. Now go do you and put this groovy cotton up your body."

Next up are pads. Pads are not cool. I know because I wear pads, and I'm embarrassed about it. It is a little niblet I whisper to women whom I want to like me better, because it is sharing a very big secret. "I don't wear tampons. I wear pads." Whoever she is, she twitches her nose up. "Oh my God, aren't they like diapers???" Yes, I say. But think of the simple technology. Babies have been wearing them for years, and mostly, they have worked. I appreciate the *comfort* of pads because I know I am involuntarily leaking blood out of my lower half, and I'd really like to feel something is there stopping it. Something like a tiny mattress, even. "I will teach you how to use a tampon!" the harborer of my secret inevitably declares, and just like that, we become best friends. I never take her up on the offer, and I continue wearing the diapers.

But besides pantyliners, which you buy because you are in moderate denial about your period being over or you accidentally leak when you laugh, there is no product more embarrassing to purchase than a product that relates to sex. Pregnancy tests, Plan B, Microgestin pills, all of it feels like ordering a cocktail at a dive bar. "I have the right to be here, but it feels so horrible!" I say to a variety of bearded people while eating the maraschino cherry off my mudslide.

I'm not saying this to be confessional or intimate with you. It's just true. It's across-the-board true. If you don't think it's embarrassing, let me ask you: Would you rather trip and fall in front of a bunch of strangers or get your birth control solely from some dude wearing a baseball cap? Would you rather fart in public or have to ride the subway with Plan B on your lap, for all to see? Isn't it weird that real embarrassing moments and your medical needs are in the same category? Take a moment to think about this. The only thing that should ever be embarrassing is what you actually listen to on your Spotify—not letting people know you protect yourself during or after sex!

I guess this is the consequence of being born in a Puritan nation. After all these years, there's still an odd stigma with women and *their* bodies. Just saying, "It's that time of the month" to people is still a "wait for them to stop pantomiming throwing up" sore spot. I could not be any more confused about this! When people have gas or a stomachache, I take it as nothing more than an affliction of being human. Same with periods. I see no reason why it's any different from announcing to the table you have a paper cut. Both are facts of life. Both involve blood. Both insinuate you are a living human being and not an alien or a robot. Still, it's guaranteed that a young man will greet me with a "blecccch" noise and say, "Too much information!" Let me level with you. "Too much information" is not simply saying, "I feel a little tired today. I am on my period." Too much information is (a) "There are clots of blood because my uterus walls are collapsing and the result looks like canned cranberry sauce in my underwear." Too much information is also (b) your description of the large dump you are about to bestow on the toilet. A rule: the announcement of body functions can be tactful as long as you don't go into detailed descriptions about them.

Periods are one thing. Birth control, that is, stopping a baby in its tracks even if the tracks aren't really built yet, is another story entirely. If you think you can't mention a period in a dinner conversation in mixed company, then try to multiply it tenfold if you talk about birth control. When I first started taking birth control, I didn't tell my parents right away. I barely mentioned it to anyone, except to girlfriends who I knew were already on it. I didn't even keep it in my purse, half because I worried I would get mugged and lose it, and half because I didn't want people to see it in my bag. I still feel weird about letting the world know I take active measures to prevent pregnancy. Why? I'm a liberated woman. I get drunk and talk about blow jobs with my friends, but there's still a part of me that doesn't want to initiate conversations about sex with people I don't know or don't trust. I know people have their opinions about harlots like me. So I keep the birth control at home, away from any wandering eyes.

Of course, I wasn't always on birth control. Birth control was, like, Plan C.

First, there were mistakes. First, there was Plan B.

Nine Months Earlier

My new boyfriend and I were quite happy and quite monogamous. I disgusted a great number of my friends with our blossoming relationship. Smiling like Cheshire cats with whole rats in their mouths. Kissing before one of us went to the bathroom. The word "babe" entering my vocabulary in a very real way. It's horrible and gross and very sublime.

Honestly, I will spare you the details, but I told him I was sweaty on our first date and he laughed and I haven't felt more comfortable in somebody's presence since. Okay, so I am not sparing you, but I was newly in love and spared nobody. Sorry.

It was also the time of our relationship when ripping things off comes into play—clothes, skirts, tights, panties, mismatched socks that you actually wore three days in a row because you needed to do laundry. We were excited and hungry in two ways: hungry in the food way because we went on lots of pasta dates, and hungry in the sex way. I wanted him all the time, which surprises me because I do not like the way condoms smell (not to ruin your sex life but they smell like all the dolls you used to play with as a kid). We spent a lot of time with our legs wrapped neatly around each other, on account of how nicely they fit.

One time, after a particularly boring house party at my apartment, we played Taboo with a bunch of other couples.

Looking back, I see this display of whiteness is overwhelming. Also looking back, I should point out that it is alienating to make other people play board games with a new couple. It makes everybody defensive of their own relationships. One couple was my roommate and his boyfriend, who had been gay their whole lives and gay for each other nearly as long. They were bored when they had to impress others with how well they knew each other. It was no longer a thing to fawn over. The second couple was in an open relationship, so they were extra happy and had a lot of trouble keeping their answers straight. The third couple was that sexy cocktail of being both boring and rude. The awful guy was too drugged out to play with his equally awful drugged-out girlfriend, who simply added to the whiteness of the room by choosing to sport blond dreadlocks. Needless to say, with our large quantity of enthusiasm and everybody else's state of boredom, my boyfriend and I could have taken over the world! Instead, we chose to enthusiastically win at Taboo.

Fresh off our victories, we bid everyone good night and retired to the bedroom. I am ashamed to say our deep sense of superiority on the board game front led to throes of passion. In this modern age, we have no great battles and no great war

(*Fight Club* quote???). We have mild victories and crushing economic strife. We have sex.

Trojan, we have a problem.

I did not feel or hear the condom rip. It wasn't until I saw his face that I knew. His face was exactly the kind of face you think would be made when the plane is crashing, when your parents saw the porn on your computer, when worst-case scenario meets consequence and the condom breaks.

To me, this was all very unfair. I had *always* used condoms, on account of the fact that they were supposed to work. If they weren't going to work, I would have spared myself the circus of searching underneath my bed for one! I wouldn't use them if they didn't work! (Note: Usually they work. Please use them all the time, every time.)

My first reaction after that moment of realization was that it was my fault. My deep woman cave must have some icicles or spikes in it that ripped the foolproof material. I went into the bathroom and felt the familiar waves of "used woman." The used woman plays the blame game, but the only contender is herself. The used woman feels bad about her body and her choices. The used woman goes to the bathroom and splashes water on her face to get all the tears off. It was, unfortunately, a familiar emotion:

I felt used in college, when a guy I was seeing called me a bitch because my best friend didn't also want to sleep with him. I felt used when I had sex with somebody who didn't call me back but broadcasted to everyone that we had sex. I felt used when somebody called me baby and then ignored me for weeks. And I felt it now, once again, after having consensual sex with a man I loved. The only link between these incidents was shame for enjoying the pleasures of the flesh and being the only one who felt its effects.

My boyfriend was extremely supportive of the whole "situation." (Side note: When you can find somebody who is supportive of things that need to be put in quotes, refuse to let that person ever leave.) Support, however, was something I didn't really need. I don't think you need somebody else to be supportive about the decisions you have to make about your own body. The condom breaks, you need a Plan B, and in this case, it was to take Plan B. There was no real decision making for me in this process, no moral waffling.

The next morning, I woke up and felt like I deserved a bacon, egg, and cheese. Whenever I want a bacon, egg, and cheese it's because I am so hungover I feel like the walls are vibrating, or because I need comfort. While I might have *said* I was okay taking Plan B, the hot cheese and Sriracha running down my face indicated otherwise.

No matter how enlightened I thought I was, obviously something was seeping into my brain that made me think I was doing something wrong. I never felt guilty enough to *not* have sex, but somehow when I was presented with the *consequences* of having sex, it made me question my own human worth. I know what kind of woman I was to some people. This is a weird feeling that is also very true: if you are a woman and you have sex, you also know what some people think of you, and it is often a series of very bad thoughts. I didn't think having sex was bad, but it was the act of acknowledging it in the light of day that made me feel guilty.

In the back of the drugstore, I stopped at the greeting cards section and slipped a glitzy ring I wore on my thumb to my ring finger. It was a move I wasn't planning. I usually wear one or two rings on my fingers, not so much as accessories, but as things I can twirl and drop on the floor and have distract me from pretty much any human contact. And when I was moving the ring from finger to finger, I stopped at my ring finger, and I kept it there. I kept it there because I was an actress, suddenly. I was buying Plan B because I was married to my husband, and we weren't ready to have children just yet. I wasn't just buying Plan B because I was in my early twenties and couldn't afford a child, couldn't even fathom what it would be like to afford a child, and still barely felt responsible for my own well-being. I wanted to be the kind of person the world would excuse, just this once, for buying Plan B before she went to work at a vintage clothing shop in order to pay her bills.

I am very ashamed of this. Now, I would barge in and just buy the damn thing, but that was not the case this time. I am telling you how desperate I was to feel validated. I am telling you how *scary* it can feel.

The lady at the register, of course, barely noticed my face, let alone my ring. Sometimes, I feel like I am fighting an invisible presence, an enemy that could be around the corner if I just turned around. This was not the day some man jumped out and ostracized me for being a scarlet whore (although I get that all the time on the Internet). The pharmacist merely took my fifty dollars and I left. Fifty dollars! Products for women, the joke begins, are so expensive. Bras. Lipstick that stays put. A wealth of gooey hair products. Medication that delivers a gut punch of hormones to your baby-makers. The only other time I made a fifty-dollar mistake was when I bought a velvet minidress at Topshop. Yikes!

I went home, got into my softest pajamas, made myself a spot of tea, and I settled in for a long winter's pseudo-abortion.

There was nothing about what I was doing that was wrong in the moral, legal, or physical sense. But it just felt . . . bad, like at any given moment, radical conservatives would burst through my door and start spitting into my eyes. "Witch!" they would shout at me. "Oy!" I would say. "Is there any decision a woman can make, even in her own house, that isn't fodder for the public?" Ann Coulter would come into the picture, shooting arrows dipped in arsenic at me. I have become the problem. I *am* the problem, I imagined the conservatives would say. Years ago, I was the person they were trying to protect. Now, my body is made to be a hole for the baby angels to live in. Do anything to compromise those little Precious Moments and you have become the enemy. Even though I was sitting on my couch, alone, reading the funny pages of the first newspaper I had bought in years. I knew I had become one of the many faceless women that, according to a lot of news sources, are part of the Great American Morality Problem. The higher the hair, the closer to God. The higher the artificial hormones, the closer to Satan. And here I am, conservative America: I have sex because I am an *adult* and I guess I fucked it up this time!

The fun thing about Plan B is, at the very least, it has the decency to make you feel as bad physically as you do mentally for taking it. You see, around hour two, my uterus began to tear my body apart. Sorry. I'm exaggerating. The vomit was tearing my body apart. Plan B was not a fun pill to take—I see no signs of it becoming the next Molly. I sat upward in the only position I could manage, wondering when I would feel the barrage of hormones leave my body. Wondering when all that was left would be me.

Still: I couldn't help but feel, in the pit of my stomach where the baby angels should be, that I deserved every moment of discomfort.

Six Months Later

After the Plan B incident, I decided it was time to go on the birth control pill. And let me tell you, it was a revelation. It shouldn't be called BIRTH CONTROL. It should be called PERIOD REGULATOR or PILL FROM HEAVEN. The term "birth control" alludes to only one of the things this magic little tablet does. It stops the babies, but it can also make your life better.

If you have periods like I do and like many women do, a birth control pill is a tiny round pill sent by Mother Earth Goddess to bless her sisters, a Mother Earth Goddess that I bet looks like Cher. "Painful" would be a word to describe my pre-birth-control period, but "crippling" might be more accurate. I cannot sufficiently describe to you the waves of sharp, constant, throbbing pain. You become an animal, a deer with its foot caught in the trap. The cramps make you crave nothing but relief. If periods were just blood, tears, and chocolate—the thing that everybody has boiled them down to—that would be one thing, but they are not. They have made me pass out in the shower. They have made stronger women than I curl up on the floor of public transport. They are nothing like your worst hangover: they are more savage, less forgiving, and have no true endpoint. When I was sixteen, I had a cyst removed from my spinal cord, which left a hole in my back that had to be stuffed with tissue and left open while it healed. On the pain scale, that was only a notch above my worst cramps.

A close friend of mine never takes sick days, but she does take period days. You can work sick, she says. You can't work during a bad period. I know this to be true and I wish I would have thought of that, too, so I wouldn't have had to lie down in an employee bathroom doubled over in pain, cheek pressed against the cool tile floor while I counted how many minutes I had left on my break.

Yet we suffer every month. But we do not have to, and here is where the magic of this little pill comes in. Obviously, using birth control pills to prevent pregnancy is a noble and correct way of using them. However, there are all sorts of other benefits that you don't hear about often, namely that they can make women happier and in *less pain*. If anybody had told me, in health class or through word of mouth, that I could control this pain with a simple pill? I would have kissed them or called them a liar.

The first two months on birth control pills, however, sucked for me. I call these first two months "the time I turned into a living *Cathy* comic." Honestly, I was the most emotional I've ever been. I felt like I didn't recognize myself. I sent back a dish at a restaurant, something that I think is against everything I've ever written in my Passive-Aggressive Commandments. I went into a bathroom and tried not to cry because somebody told me Hillary Clinton would not make a good president. I'm not even a giant Clinton FAN. I got angry at my boyfriend and my mother for doing annoying things like breathing. I was on an emotional roller coaster, and when the amusement park workers took my picture on the big cliff down, it would have shown me eating a giant cake, crying. However, after a few good weeks of good-ole-fashioned horror, hark! A light! I liken it to the castle in *Beauty and the Beast* turning from stone to marble once Belle's Stockholm syndrome kicked in enough to break the curse. My skin cleared. My mood cleared. My breasts got larger. *Birth control pills are great*, I thought!

Then I didn't get my period for three months.

For this round of "things that aren't working that are supposed to work," I blame the instructions. Birth control instructions are very vague. The people over at Microgestin FE knew that I wanted to get it on with my man, but like the concerned parent in a sitcom, they were going to make it a bit difficult for me.

There's a name for a person like me, and it's called a "Sunday Starter." That is not a football term. That is the name of somebody who "starts Microgestin FE on the first Sunday after your period starts, even if you are still having your period." But I had already gotten my period a week before, so I just started it on a regular Monday. Starting pills on a Monday still makes me a Sunday Starter, but not really, because my period was already done. Categorically, this just makes me a "Starter." Confused yet?

The pack suggests that I do not need other contraceptives for seven days after the Sunday start, but because I was not a Sunday Starter, I wasn't sure what that meant. I told my boyfriend, "I think we should wait a bit to stop using condoms." He said, "How long?" and I said, "Maybe eight years." I called my gynecologist but she didn't pick up and then I chickened out about calling back. So I checked the Internet, which said things ranging from "maybe you'll be okay" to racist troll comments on birth control forums.

Out of all the things I've mentioned so far about my life, I am most embarrassed to admit that I was too ashamed to have a talk with my doctor. Talking with your doctor is recommended on all commercials about medicine. You can ask your doctor anything. As a society, we really encourage a healthy dialogue between patient and medical professional. Yet the idea of calling only to ask her when it was okay for me to house semen in my body safely and without consequence seemed awful. I didn't want to do it, so instead, I said after nine days, "I think it should be fine now," and then I didn't get my period for three months.

The second thing that embarrassed me, of course, is this: yo, use a condom even if you are on birth control, even if you are in a committed relationship. Like, I know that I was greedy and excited about being monogamous and potentially could live in a world without that weird gross plastic scent, but relax. Be safe.

When month one rolled around with no period, in the earliest stages of uncertainty, I got to be philosophical and thinky with the not-yet-plausible concept of potentially being pregnant.

As a woman and human being, I have always been "pro-choice." I feel like people aren't too clear about the word "choice." It means options. I believe pro-choice does not mean "Abort everything! Abort living children! Abort! Who cares, let's just cook and eat 'em!" I believe pro-choice means that terminating a pregnancy is a surgical procedure. The decision to have a surgical procedure should be made by the sound-minded person who would be having the procedure. I believe pro-choice means that if you get pregnant and are deeply Catholic and do not believe in abortion, you should not have to get one. If you are atheist or Catholic or raped or asexual or short or hate children or tall or a goddamn centaur and you want an abortion you should have access to one.

I'm not here to argue whether or not you believe a fetus, in its unborn state, is a person. If you do, don't get an abortion. Just don't take away my right to one. When I see people picketing outside Planned Parenthood, a large part of me wonders how much these people value *all* human life. If they did, would they support war? Do they support the death penalty? Do they cry when children in other countries die? Do they believe in all life, or just restricting mine?

There are a couple of fallacies that come with the idea of abortion. One of them is that the people who have them are either monsters or, in rare cases, tragic women who were put in awful positions. You have no idea why somebody wants to get an abortion. It shouldn't matter. There is this idea of "good" abortions—abortions from rape or incest or risk to life. But some women just have abortions because they can't have a baby, for whatever reason that might be. I don't want to paint stories of the women whom we will sympathize with. I want to paint the story that all women should have the right to access the health care and the medical attention and the *information* they need if they desire to have a surgical procedure. Another fallacy is that if we ban abortions, they will stop. They will not. My mother grew up in a world where people crossed state lines to have illegal abortions. Believe me, laws will not stop anything but the safety, security, and the protection of a lot of women in this country.

As a sexually active woman, there is always a release of breath when you get your period on time, every time. But when that moment is delayed, you retreat to that thought in the back of your mind: what would I do? You have mulled over scenarios, tested your mettle, and come up with a stance. You aren't sure if this stance will be the decision when you are actually on the battlefield. But it feels reasonable to come up with one, just in case. And now, I was the closest I'd ever been to having to make that decision myself.

So, if I am pregnant, SHOULD I have an abortion? Those first few weeks, I battled a lot of different scenarios in the darkest game of "Would you rather?" Would you rather halt your life for an unplanned child? Are you ready for your life to change either way? As a person who ping-pongs between the logic of agnosticism and the hope that maybe I will go to a fluffy cloud place when I die, a part of me worried that if I went through with the procedure, I would carry guilt with me for the rest of my life. I know because I already felt guilty just *thinking* about it. I feel a great pain for women who have to go through this. It is not an easy choice, even if it *is* an easy decision. It is something you will always remember.

In college, the idea of an abortion was pretty much a no-brainer to me. I was young and too unhinged to take care of a friend's goldfish, let alone a child. I had my whole future ahead of me to become all the things I would one day be, and an unplanned pregnancy didn't jive with those plans. But now, at twenty-four, I was unsure. On paper, I was aware that it was perfectly reasonable for me to have a baby. This was one of the healthiest years, physically, for me to breed. Circumstance-wise, I was also in a pretty okay spot. I was with a man whom I could see myself being with for the long haul. He was healthy and had hair on his head. I had a career, the resourcefulness to make money when I needed it, and a maturity that only comes with age. I had two parents who would embrace grandparent-life with open arms and an open house.

So, if I was pregnant and didn't have the baby, it was only because I didn't WANT TO have a child. And deep down in the pit of my stomach, I knew I did not want to. I just wasn't ready. I still wanted to have nights out drinking and wearing tights with rips. I still wanted to travel to Italy and eat *cacio e pepe* without kids or a babysitter. I still wanted to be reckless and young. I didn't want to worry about another life. Even if I was getting tired at eleven p.m., I still wanted to live a lot, write at two a.m., and chug wine out of the bottle. It would be a selfish decision.

So yes, I decided. I SHOULD have an abortion, should the test tell me that I was pregnant. I had to go with my gut, and my gut said it wasn't ready to share space with a baby. In this situation, I was pro-choice, and I would be pro-consequence, too.

When month two came without a period, I began to ask myself the harder question: COULD I have an abortion? To think about it as a possibility is one thing. This time, I had to think about it in real time. If a doctor told me I was pregnant, would I fall in love with it immediately? Would I feel the same joy my mother did when she found out she was pregnant with me? Would I feel a connection I just couldn't shake? If push comes to shove, I had to wonder if I could find it in myself to go to a clinic.

I didn't know if it would be easy, but I knew that I could do it if I had to. I knew that I would feel unbearably sad because I already felt sad. But I knew that I could make a doctor's appointment, put on a flimsy hospital robe, and have a procedure. I knew that I could do it because when I thought about it, it was the only thing that felt like an answer.

When month three arrived dry, I couldn't take the constant back-and-forth of weighing out the theoretical anymore. And now we're back to the beginning. I'm eating Reese's Puffs and pondering the complexities of life.

I wasn't pregnant. It was a huge, huge relief.

I cried. I cried because I was relieved. I cried because it worked out how I wanted. I cried because I had looked up abortion clinics already, and I knew where they were. I cried because I didn't have to do what I know I would have done.

If that test had shown up differently, if it were a YES instead of a NO, I do think that I would have gotten an abortion. I would have done it swiftly, and sadly, but I would not have regretted it.

In all the shame a woman experiences, in all the matters in which her body is supposed to be controlled, in all the ways society tries to tell her what she is doing is wrong, she will always have feelings about it. But the important thing to remember is that no matter what that feeling is, it is *your* feeling and it is *your* decision. You own those. Getting an abortion might have made me sad. I might have cried for days. I might have felt nothing and went partying the next night. You might not be sad about it. You might feel fine, and that's not bad either. It's not the reaction that we need to fight for; it's the decision. But I wouldn't have regretted it. I would have been grateful for the life I would get to have because of it.

When it boils down to it, there shouldn't be any judgment on *how* a person decides what to do with her body. I trust that women will find a way, no matter what the choice. We will always find a way to raise the baby we want to have, through counting pennies and sacrificing free time and sleep. If we don't want to have that baby, we will travel states and cities and towns to find the help we need. We are resourceful. We are headstrong.

There is a way, I believe, to get rid of the shame. It is by open dialogue. It is by saying to somebody you have your period and rebutting when the person starts to retch. It is by putting Plan B on the top of the cart for all to see. It is by keeping your birth control in plain sight. It is by telling people that your decisions are yours, and then making peace with those decisions. It is by remembering every day that people are trying to take our right to choose away. Every single day, clinics are getting shut down, resources dwindle, and women are left alone and with no options. We have to remember this every single day. We have to fight this every single day.

After all, we have no great war. No great battle. We only have sex.

We must also have our choice. We *will* have our choice.

Your Beauty Is Magic:
On Loving My Face

After decades of living with my own face, there is nothing you could say about my appearance that would shock me. There's no insult you could hurl, no compliment you could offer, that I haven't already told myself. To me, these subjective judgments are facts: My front teeth are spaced out and sort of uneven. My eyes are big and my eyebrows thicker. My lips are small. However, that doesn't stop people from offering me unsolicited advice on my appearance. Instead of just letting me walk around, medium attractiveness and all, people will suggest things. *You should think about getting contacts. It would look better. You would see your eyes more!* I'm not an *idiot*, I want to say. I *know* I would look amazing in contacts, too, but I don't wash my hands enough to risk touching my eyeballs so often. When somebody lets me know they liked my hair longer, or I would be beautiful if I dyed it lighter, or that the lipstick I am wearing is too much, I want to scream something along the lines of: What more do you want from me? Do you have a paper bag I could put lipstick on and prance around in? They are being helpful, they think, *to this poor girl who doesn't know about her face, to this poor girl who doesn't know how to make herself look better.*

Take my use of makeup, for instance. I *love* wearing a lot of makeup. I'm talking "as subtle as Dolly Parton" levels, here. People are horrified, very truly horrified about this. They have to help me, they think. *Take some of it off! You would look better in warmer colors! Do something! Do anything! Haven't you ever thought about trying a neutral lip?*

And the advice comes from all sorts of people. Older women tell me that I shouldn't wear makeup to cover up my beautiful face. One time I was in the bathroom at my old job and somebody came in and said, "Well, you looked better with *yesterday's* lipstick." Many different men like to let me know that "honestly, men like it when you wear less makeup." Okay. Well, I liked it when Khal Drogo wore less eyeliner, but you wouldn't see me visiting his deathbed to tell him that. I do get a fair amount of niceties, from women who are enthusiastic about my eyebrow shape or contour, but a lot of the time, I hear this:

"You look so pretty without makeup!"

"Maybe," I say. "But *I like it this way.*"

Also, you *say* I look prettier without makeup, but I know plenty of women who do not wear makeup. They are straight up accosted with makeup advice. They are chased around with the mascara suggestions that will improve their eyelashes and their lives. They are told often how just a touch of bronze on the cheeks will make their whole face glow. Maybe if I went over and rubbed my face, chock-full of foundation and primer and gunk, on these women's faces, and half of it stayed on my face and the other half went on all the makeup-less lady faces, the world would be happy. Apparently, there is some magic "proper amount of stuff to put on your face" ratio that I haven't found yet, but the truth remains, you simply cannot leave the house without somebody telling you how you might look better doing something else. There's always room for improvement.

The thing about this is that I have very little interest in being a natural beauty. I prefer to look slightly *unnatural*. I wear a lot of makeup for a few reasons, but these reasons have changed over the years. I like the ritual of putting makeup on. I like the fact that I can do a lot of different things with it. I like that I can change my facial features just slightly. I can make my cheekbones a little more chiseled, my eyebrows a bit shapelier, my eyes a bit sparklier. A lot of the time, I can confidently look in the mirror and say I am beautiful. Makeup helps me feel beautiful. I think I am beautiful.

There. I said it. Was that sort of weird? Do you ever call your face beautiful? What do you think you feel more comfortable with—listing your physical flaws or saying you are beautiful? I mean, I've seen Dove commercials. I think we have our answer.

I am pretty aware of all my flaws, mostly because I've pointed them out to myself. It's not all Regina George ego over here. Oh God, I have so many flaws to list. For starters, I think my nose is too fat. Not too big but too *wide*. When I was nine years old, I used to want a nose job. I wised up, of course—by twenty-two, I prayed I would get a "deviated septum" and let insurance pay to fix it. I think my nose, at certain angles, makes me look like an old British man in a Dickens remake. Sometimes I stare at it and want it to go straight back to whatever old man is running around on BBC, and to be replaced with a little ski slope or an elvish kind of thing. I think the pores on my nose and chin are much too large. I feel at times that those dots look like the aerial view of a city. My eyelashes are long, but I do not have enough of them. When I get my period, I get breakouts on the side of my face. Often, I pick at these breakouts till they bleed and I have a brand-new set of problems. Like the problem that I am well past puberty and still get pimples, but hey, life sucks and then we all die, I guess. Oh! And my chin is too angular in certain pictures. Also, it is not symmetrical. Surely you have heard about how important that is for the face! I take a lot of issue with the lack of symmetry in my face. But this all gets rather tiresome. I've already done myself the favor of insulting myself about my looks every which way. I've done this for much of my life, in greater heaps than any bully has ever done for me. I've actually apologized for the way I look when I wake up or without foundation. I'm not alone in this. I don't know why many of us do it—maybe it's because we're mad we don't look a certain way. Or maybe it's because we're mad we're *supposed* to look a certain way. Whatever it is, it's exhausting. It takes a lot longer to reach this place than it does to simply hate yourself all day, but once you let yourself be beautiful sometimes, living with your face is a hell of a lot easier. So that's what I decided to do.

I think I'm beautiful. Not every second, but sometimes. There are moments I can just revel in the beauty of my face, because if I didn't, I would go completely nuts. It's much more harmonious to be a little bit of a narcissist. My brain is much happier for it. My iPhone is full of pictures of my dogs, about thirty photos of oozing cheese sandwiches, and, since the invention of the selfie, all sorts of photos of me, wearing all different kinds of lipsticks. I can really love my fucking face to almost excessive levels at times.

Seriously, is this getting kind of disturbing? Is this turning you off? Is it because if you place me next to Leighton Meester, I might resemble some sort of shredded potato latke in glasses? This doesn't mean I won't put on a new lipstick, take a picture, and feel absolutely radiant. This doesn't mean I am not beautiful.

I have struggled with my own beauty for many years. Struggling with beauty is sort of a given for women. If you've ever had a casual conversation with a girl while she's getting dressed for an event, you might understand. I thought beauty was something bestowed upon you by a fairy at birth. I thought beauty was magic you couldn't harness.

After years of searching for many things, including keys, happiness, and lost bracelets, I have stumbled on a truth. It's not only helpful to allow yourself the off-putting joy of feeling beautiful, it's borderline revolutionary. Looking into the mirror and liking what you see is one of the most important and powerful things you can do for yourself. I do believe you are familiar with the idea of *Love Yourself!* shouted with vigor in body-positive soap commercials, in women's magazines, and by your mother. It's sort of Women's Lib Lite. First of all: this should be a no-brainer. You should love yourself. Of *course* you should love the *one body and face you get for all your life.* It's basic, simple human decency. Shouldn't we strive for a little more than that? Apparently, there is a journey you must take as a woman: to hate the way you look, then "embrace" the way you look when you can't physically hate it anymore. The story line remains the same. You fight your face, and through self-enlightenment, you accept it, and then you are happy. Voilà!

I followed that story line to a T.

I've never really thought I was stunning in a way that made people, like, start Trojan Wars for me or consider me for vampire movie roles. For most of my life, I gave very little credit to my face. I hated it at times, when I was swimming deep in the low-self-esteem pool, but for the most part, I just felt like I was just another girl with glasses and brown hair. You could practically throw a fitted flannel shirt into a coffee shop and find thirty girls who look just me fighting over it. I felt indifferent toward it at best.

And the older I got, the more I liked my other attributes, such as my intelligence and my ability to eat at least twenty-six meals a day, and beauty got kind of pushed to the back burner. And while that is good and very important, I denied myself the simple pleasure of looking in the mirror and liking what I saw. After all, I was born in this skin. I had to deal with it forever, and the most I could muster was a hearty:

"You know, my face isn't that bad!"

Boom! Done, right? Wrong. *Love Yourself!* is not the end of the story. It is the beginning. It is the absolute bare minimum.

I'd rather challenge you to do better.

We all struggle with the body hate, the face dislike, the constant barrage of "we should be criticizing ourselves." We never hear women declare their own beauty, even if they are beautiful by "society's standards." (Also: Imagine me doing that dismissive jack-off motion when I say "society's standards," because who falls in that category? Like *two people*? What about the rest of the world? Why can't I be normal-looking, or different-looking and still run around liking the *one face I have*? *This is not* Face/Off. *I definitely have one face and I should go around liking it.*)

I find it kind of insulting when people say that girls do not feel beautiful. I know they do, even if it's just sometimes, even if it's just a little bit, or in a certain lighting, or in a certain dress. I feel beautiful when I am alone in the bathroom and I have put my hair up just to wash my face. I feel beautiful when I am naked out of the shower and I take time to rub vanilla lotion on my legs. I feel beautiful in little glimpses of mirrors, or when I am changing, or when someone envelops me in a strong hug, or when I get a haircut. For years, I have felt beautiful in those little personal moments. I have secretly examined my face in mirrors. I privately became happy with the way my face looked.

Here's the revolution: I want you to feel beautiful, and not so secretly. Feeling beautiful doesn't mean you think you should be a supermodel: it means you like what you see when you see yourself. I want the world to be crawling with women who tell you that they think they are beautiful. I want to take all your flaws and shove them in the face of the world. I want you to say: "I don't really care what you think about it, because I think it." It takes away a little bit of that objectification that so often comes with being beautiful. And it *is* brazen. A brazen love of yourself.

You've spent all too long feeling "just enough," and only beautiful when you are alone in your room. I challenge you to look the world in the face and say you love the way you look, and that you are beautiful the way you are born and also the way you choose to look. I want you to dance to that jam. To harness this magic, you must find the thing that gives you power.

For me, this started with a lipstick. It might not be lipstick for you. But for me, it was MAC Cyber lipstick, in all its deep-purple-almost-black corpselike glory.

The first lipstick that ever made me love my face, as most firsts are, was all wrong for me. Still, it was one of the most important purchases I have made, regardless of what color it made my teeth look. I'm used to "all wrong" being a bad thing. I've worn my share of unflattering skirt lengths, viewed apartments that don't have sinks or closets, and answered job ads that use the words "upbeat" and "smiling" as part of their description. However: *the rules* do not apply for lipstick as they do for people, pencil skirts, or anything else that you need to find "the right fit" for. I know because buying unflattering fifteen-dollar lipstick might have been one of the best things that has ever happened to me.

I found myself attracted to Cyber immediately and surprisingly. When I put it on my lips, an emotion I hadn't quite associated with my face for a long time appeared, out of nowhere.

I was eleven, and I was a witch for Halloween. My mother had bought me CVS costume lipstick that came in a pack with black acrylic nails. The nails I took no interest in. Even now, I have no interest in doing my nails, because I suffer from "needing to stick my hands in bags the second I paint my nails" disorder. But the lipstick was black, and it smelled like grapes. I slathered the stuff on and ran around the house for hours, alive and primal. Usually, I wanted to stay home, let my brother go trick-or-treating, and try to bargain with him to give me all the Reese's he got. This year, I was at every house.

Cyber called to me in a similar, witchy way. It was dark and unforgiving. It called attention to your face. It screamed, "You don't have to like me." It screamed all the things I had wanted to scream for so long, but I instead chose to stay pretty, to aim for pretty, to aim for flattering.

I was not used to calling attention to my face *on purpose*. I was absolutely terrified to put the lipstick on.

At the time, I was twenty-two. I visited the MAC counter, on a hot summer day when I was off from work early. I was doing grunt assistant work for an office on Wall Street. Because of this, all my beauty wires were being crossed. Before I started working there, I was so used to Williamsburg, where beautiful was hobo layers and nipple piercings and Bettie Page bangs. On Wall Street, beauty was long legs with stilettos and matte red lips. Blow-dried hair. Impeccable suits. I looked absolutely nothing like the people there. I was like some sort of weirdo who specifically came into their lives to drop manila files in front of the boss's door, like a punch line. What was I? I was just a girl in the Nordstrom Junior's Department blazer I bought when I did a brief stint on the debate team in high school. I had never felt so out of place. These are the times, of course, that you feel like you should undergo your own make-over. A lot of the women in my life are very good at the im-promptu makeover, and I was no exception. I graduated from college and chopped off all my hair into an asymmetrical nightmare that took forever to grow out. I got dumped? I gave up carbs for one tortured week and worked out until I dropped a few pounds.

This time, I had college loans, a much more limited budget, and absolutely no desire to exercise. So I went with lipstick as a last resort, a temporary pick-me-up. For years, I thought lipstick was a truly deep pain in the ass. I was a balm girl. I didn't have time for lipstick. It smears when I am doing some of my favorite things, because some of my favorite things are eating and touch-ing my face. It gets all over you when you are kissing, or more aptly for me, wiping my face with a napkin (hand). It is hard to apply and all the colors make me exhausted. The *names* for lip-sticks make me even more exhausted. Malibu-a-go-go. Candy Yum Yum. Lady Danger. Very rarely does an actual color appear in the title of lipstick.

I had had some boring affairs with lipstick, but they were all of the brick-red and baby-pink variety. Brick Red lippie on me was the James-Marsden-in-Romantic-Comedies of lipstick colors: I can live a life of passionless satisfaction with it but there are never any real fireworks. It wasn't until I met my soul mate that things changed.

I saw the Cyber and kept picking it up. The salesperson approached me.

"You want to try it on?"

I put it down and told her that no, I was interested in a nude pink that wouldn't make me look washed out, because it was summer and dark lipstick wasn't even in style in the summer. She looked at me like I was nuts. "Why are you following styles? You should wear whatever you want, anytime. Don't follow styles, follow you." The other MAC employee looked up from arranging eye shadows and nodded, sagely, in my direction.

She applied Cyber to my lips. It washed out my face and brought attention to the fact that I hadn't waxed my mustache in a hot second, on account of how much that hurts. Men at bars would hate it. My parents would hate it. But I felt absolutely brilliant in it. I felt somewhat of a stirring in me, kind of like Meryl Streep in *The Bridges of Madison County*, but with a MAC tube instead of an old man. I felt powerful, magnificent, Maleficent. It was a new feeling. I felt power. I felt power in the way I looked, like maybe I could knock somebody down or say something like "I don't care how you do it, JUST DO IT!" I liked that, so I bought that.

I was certainly not used to wearing makeup in a way that was for my own pleasure, and not just to save me from being ugly. I think the most interesting thing I found about claiming beauty for your own is how much you can shed new light on things that you previously used against yourself. For me, makeup became something I used to wear to make me "good enough," and I made it into something that made me great.

I do have to point out how paradoxical it might seem that makeup was the boost I needed to feel beautiful. I didn't always have the greatest experience with the beauty industry. I know that a lot of women haven't, either. Until I realized there wasn't much to fix, the beauty industry was where I turned when I felt my absolute worst.

For the most part, the beauty industry is here to keep you from visibly aging, keep you hairless, and keep you looking almost the complete opposite of yourself. Willingly, we do it, because our physical features have been made fun of for decades: by classmates calling us pizza face, by commercials showing birds flying out of frizzy hair, and by the women waxing our eyebrows who try to subtly tell us they can get rid of our sideburns or mustaches, too. We've been taught that wrinkles are the Antichrist, even though the MOVIE *Antichrist* featured Willem Dafoe, who I believe is actually a human wrinkle. We women are living in fear of what horrible thing the beauty industry will tell us to be self-conscious about next, like maybe the insides of our elbows or our earlobes or the backs of our knees.

I have been a hearty consumer of the beauty industry and its many products for more than half of my time on this Earth. I was twelve years old when I shaved for the first time, and I didn't do it because I wanted to. If you haven't guessed by the number of times I've mentioned it, I am a hairy adult. I was also a very, very hairy child. I was somewhere between Austin Powers and "Disney's Beast falling on a barbershop floor, wet." My hair started sprouting up right after puberty: my eyebrows met in the middle and I had a little "Pedro from *Napoleon Dynamite*" mustache. I had soft hair on my lower back and very visible hair on my legs. Kids are pretty ruthless when it comes to body hair, which makes no sense, because it's not like we're at the age to go to a salon. The mere presence of my body hair resulted in me being called "the it" in middle school. Not only does that paint a lovely picture of the little mutants these kids were, but surely you understand why I began to try to convince my mother to let me shave my legs.

Considering my childhood (and adulthood) superpower

was managing to accidentally hurt myself on objects that didn't have any sharp edges at all, my mother was hesitant to let me near anything that could potentially destroy my veins. So I merely began to fantasize about the day when my legs would be hairless and everybody would think I was beautiful. She did, however, Nair off my mustache for me.

Do you remember when you learned that beauty is synonymous with pain? My mother learned it when somebody drove a needle through her ears as a baby. Some learn it from getting their hair relaxed for the first time. I learned it from the burning of the lip cream I used. The commercials make it seem so fun! Spoiler alert: It's not. It smells like cleaning chemicals and turns your skin hairless but bright red. Sometimes, it burns. I was embarrassed until the pain subsided and I could look like every other little girl, every little blond girl with light body hair or the girls with seemingly no hair at all.

Finally, my mother decided I could use my father's electric razor to get rid of my leg hair. I had a Herculean task at hand, to rid myself of all my body hair. Like maybe if you strapped a bunch of razors to a Roomba, it would work.

Soon after I let the razor touch my skin, making it smooth but somehow still grainy at the same time, I took tweezers from my mother's drawer. I had a Peter Gallagher–sized eyebrow in between my other two regular eyebrows, and it begged for attention. "Just the tweezers" turned into my mother's Revlon brown eyeliner, a small sample size of her Clinique moisturizer, and later, volumizing shampoo. I began to fall deep into the pit of grooming and beauty rituals, and I was addicted to the small improvements I thought they made. I wanted to be traditionally beautiful, which I wasn't, and I wanted to be beautiful so other people would think I was beautiful and want to kiss me.

The hair on my head was another source of contention for

me. I went to a predominately white school, and I very much had biracial hair: it was curly, it was crazy, it was dark, and it was out of control. Man, do ethnic girls have a wild relationship with their hair. People want to fix it or touch it, mostly. So I bought a hair straightener and a heat-protectant spray. I made it look like the hair that I thought everybody was supposed to have. I wanted to look how I thought everybody wanted me to look.

Of course, eventually, I dealt with a new kind of hair. Whenever somebody says, "Hey, we're going to go swimming, wanna come?" I get angry that the person didn't give me more notice. You don't just SLAP on a BATHING SUIT. You have to spend two hours in the bathroom first. I have to attack my bikini line with a prayer, a sharp razor, and enough shaving cream to ice around three hundred cakes. Don't be fooled by the gentle strawberry scent emanating from the bathroom. This is a serious "Code Red *Dunston Checks OUT*" kind of scenario. I need a moment or else the bottom half of my bathing suit is gonna look like those evil vines slowly climbing up into the Mayan temple during that movie *The Ruins*.

But never fear. As those old beauty-industry folks say, "There's a serum for that."

For years, I mostly used all these products because I felt like I had to. It wasn't out of vanity, or an incredible need to spend all my money; it was out of fear. I had been made fun of before for things I could have fixed; I wasn't going to get myself in that same predicament ever again. I shivered thinking that someone might find out how completely average and splotchy my skin looks without the assistance of acne cream. I was terrified someone would discover how flat my hair looks without volumizing mousse, or how full my mustache is without waxing. I looked at my face and hair and skin like a floor I had to completely cover up with carpet. A lot of the time things like "putting time into your appearance" can be thought of as vapid and vain. I never felt that way. I felt too scared at what would happen if I didn't.

And then, I got very, very tired of hating myself.

As a feminist, I've always felt guilty about wanting to look nice or conventionally pretty. How do I know I'm doing it for myself and not for the man, or what we've been taught is the way we should look? That's something I can't really answer. I don't know if I like the pinup aesthetic because it was created by cosmetic companies to make women buy more makeup. I don't know if I like heavy smoky eyes because some magazine said it was the sexiest. All I know is that I *chose* it. Not because I thought it would look the best, but because I liked it the most.

Now, don't get me wrong. I still use and purchase some of the exact same products I used to buy, and I still probably spend a similar amount of money on them. They currently clutter up my drawers, small travel bags on top of my drawers, and are wont to hide underneath my bed just when I need them. I have translucent powders and foundation powders, and the fluffy brushes needed to apply them. I have a light concealer to brighten my undereyes and a darker one to conceal redness. I have different kinds of blushes to imitate a variety of things (glow from inside, just had sex, came back in from the cold). I have foundations for when I'm tan, not tan, and sort of tan, and mascara that is lengthening, mascara that is volumizing, mascara that is supposed to look like no mascara, and mascara that has a smaller brush for my bottom lashes. I have bronzer to warm up my face and a cooler shade to contour. I have brightening primers and blurring primers, highlighters in champagne and highlighters in rose pink, liquids and powders and liquid-to-powders, and enough copper eye shadow to turn about two hundred dimes into pennies. I have black lipstick and invisible lip liner and rosy lip gloss, brow pencils and pomades and gels, long-lasting matte lip cream and ChapStick, and enough products to fill up, well, maybe one-forty-fifth of a Sephora.

But I *like* every product I buy, and I've thought about every product I've bought, and I love the way every product makes me feel. And that's the power of it to me.

Women have always known there is power in the way they look—but most of the time it feels like a passive thing, a handing over of power rather than one we can harness. Magazines tell you *when* to have curly hair or what kind of hair men want you to have. They tell you the sexy bikini-wax trends and the exact type of makeup to wear on a date. With some practice, you can be your best self, which is Kim Kardashian or Beyoncé . . . when Kimmy K was thinner and didn't have baby weight or cellulite, or when Beyoncé was Photoshopped to have lighter skin. Be Beyoncé—who isn't really Beyoncé! It's exactly what men (i.e., the men who own the companies that sell us shit) like! I have seen countless polls that ask men what they like on women, but I've never seen a poll asking women what they like on women. We rarely feel like the decision makers of our own aesthetic.

This is important: to find out what you truly like in your own aesthetic, even if it goes against the grain of perfection. Maybe you don't want to hide your freckles or lose five pounds, or maybe you like your hair natural. Maybe you like dressing in big stripes or crop tops even though you're bigger! As for me, I like wearing obnoxiously bright lipstick. Deep purple, orange, neon pink, true red, you name it, I slather it all over my lips.

Finding something that I loved absolutely shattered the way I felt about beauty and grooming. You have to understand that I am not just shouting the power of makeup to you. I am shouting the power of finding the things that reflect your aesthetic, and brandishing those, and feeling beautiful in those choices.

Declaring your beauty is revolutionary, not only because you deserve to feel it, but because you deserve for everyone around you to know it. You deserve to dictate it. You deserve for it to be a part of your personality because there are so many other wonderful parts of your personality that make it a whole.

Pretty is great, and so is kind, interesting, fiery, ambitious, khaleesi, funny, smart, and a million more things. Be all of them. You deserve to like yourself, every single part of yourself, and think it is all beautiful.

And don't forget to check your teeth for lipstick before you go out. That's just smart thinking.

Top Ten Makeup Tips I Can Give You:

1. Everybody looks good in red lipstick. Keep trying. For a perfect classic red, you have to buy Sephora's Cream Lip Stain in shade 01. It's under twenty bucks and will last you through three slices of pizza and a makeout session.

2. To perfect your cat eye, realize that you will never truly perfect your cat eye. Keep practicing and be satisfied with a bit of unevenness every once and a while. Try a felt tip pen from Stila or e.l.f. and be amazed at how much easier application is with one of those babies.

3. For perfect foundation, buy a good foundation brush. I love Real Techniques Expert Face Brush, but a Beautyblender also works great. And match

your foundation by putting it directly on your jaw-
line in the most fluorescent of lights.

4. In the same vein, good-quality brushes will make
   shitty makeup a million times more workable. You
   must own a good foundation brush, a good blush
   brush, and a good eye shadow blending brush.
   Clean those brushes.

5. The best lipstick combination in the world is MAC
   Nightmoth Pencil and MAC Diva lipstick. I refuse
   to believe anything else.

6. Layer mascaras. Find a great volumizing mascara
   and find a good lengthening mascara and double
   those babies up. You will rarely need false lashes,
   which I cannot do anyway because I wear glasses
   and therefore it looks like a caterpillar on a wind-
   shield.

7. Spend money on: foundation, concealer, and skin
   care. You can always buy cheap lipstick, mascara,
   and eyeliner.

8. If you have tired eyes, buy a concealer shade one
   tone lighter than your regular skin color, draw an
   upside-down triangle on your face, and use your
   ring finger to blend.

9. For bright eyes, nude eyeliner in the waterline is
   also a lifesaver.

10. Do whatever the fuck you want, wear whatever
    you want, and don't let anybody tell you that you
    look better any other way.

Where Have You Been All My Life?
(An Ode to Female Friendships)

If you are one of those girls who think they don't get along with other women, I implore you to hang out in bar bathrooms more. It is the only thing about New York City nightlife I love.

It's eleven p.m. on a Friday night and I'm stuck in hell. Hell, to me, is any crowded bar or club in New York City. Any of them. Even the ones you promise me are your favorite and the bartenders are cute and the drinks are really strong. Even the ones you promise me don't get crowded, ever. It's a lie. They do. Just because I can't see past my hand, bathed in neon-red lighting like we're in a dream sequence, doesn't mean I can't feel a sea of men and women willing to pay twelve bucks a cocktail to convince themselves they are having a good time. I feel them because they are sweaty, and because they are pressing themselves against me on the way to opening up a tab. We are not having a good time. We are simply festering, under heat lamps, waiting to hatch into the kinds of chicks that don't need to go to bars anymore.

This particular bar, on this particular night, is in the Meatpacking District, where you have to walk through cobblestoned streets to arrive at bars where men dipped in name-brand cologne stand outside, the men of the wall, smoking cigarettes. It's a minefield to get through those streets, even for somebody who thinks thick wedges are "heels enough." I am going to celebrate a friend's birthday, a friend who has reached that panicky New York City age when you get worried that you aren't living fabulously and extravagantly enough, so you throw a birthday party in a place that the devil coughed up: a lounge. Not quite bar and not quite club, except for the worst parts of both—the alcohol is expensive yet comes in flimsy plastic cups, with lime garnishes that have been passed through the hands of so many aspiring actor/bartenders, they might as well be the phone numbers of Bravo casting directors. The music is loud. It sounds like a human glowstick. And there are couches, which remind you of the sweet respite of home, which is a twenty-five-dollar ride away in a cab driven by a cabbie who doesn't want to take you to Brooklyn. These couches, however, do not have remote controls and blankets on them. They have seen more vomit and gyrations than we ever will.

To show support and camaraderie, I have dressed up in one of the only LBD club outfits I have. It is three years old, but still tight in the right places, so therefore dubbed a "classic," or "Vintage Forever 21." I went through this horrible phase when I was twenty-three in which I decided I would be part of the Friday night/Saturday night scene. I bought a handful of bodycon dresses, a teasing comb, and lip gloss. My affair was brief, because I realized that snaking my way through sweaty crowds of people was only appealing in my fantasy world, where I was an elf and they were orcs, and I could stab them with a sword.

And now I am back here, a reminder of how bad I was at

dating and dancing, because I *am trying very hard to be a good friend*. I am always working on *being a good friend*. I love my friends dearly, but I am notorious for dropping off the radar, and forgetting to call back, and becoming somewhat of a hermit, and many are not tolerant of this. I make up for it by getting them drunk on the giant bottles of wine I always keep in my house and getting them incredible birthday and Christmas presents, which makes me feel like a deadbeat father on television. So I show up in the dress and make face because I am trying to be a better person who goes to all birthday parties. Birthday parties are a good start. Going to events even though I have the kind of social anxiety that makes me speak to myself in a bathroom mirror is one of my "being a good friend" moments.

I enter the bar after triumphantly showing my ID to a bouncer, a Goliath teddy bear who almost seems as horrified as I am, behind the eyes. I plow my way to a reserved table. Hugs abound. My hair, swaddled in so much hair spray you could no doubt shove an infant in it and have it survive the Oregon Trail, is already wilting like a deflated birthday balloon. My makeup, which nobody in the world would call restrained, is mightily slipping down my face like I am Queen Bey in the "Why Don't You Love Me" video.

After saying my hellos and giving halfhearted hugs to acquaintances, I shove my way to the bartender and try not to make eyes at any one man for a second, in case he is a Turtle from *Entourage* type. I am like a magnet to the stockier male friends of more attractive people, the ones with the kind of facial hair that could only be marketed as "unfortunate." I am the stockier female friend of much more attractive women, and Turtles believe we can bond in some way, sexually, over this.

Honestly, I'm never flattered. I hate making small talk, and

I hate meeting people. As much as I want to respond to every opening line with the high-pitched wailing of *La Llorona*, I usually just smile and nod. Which is worse. To this day, I think bars should hand out wristbands for people who have to go to birthdays but don't specifically want to talk to anybody.

Three drinks in, three drinks hard-won and drunk while nodding at friends because I can't hear them and don't want to make them repeat themselves, and I have to pee. I have the bladder of an already wet, small sponge, and so does every other woman in New York, apparently. The line snakes around the block. I don't mind, though, because I'm about to enter the one mecca, the one lifesaver, the best part about going to the bar: the women's bathroom.

The women's bathroom is a utopia of sorts. The rules of society do not apply here. If men are worried that women will one day be able to breed without them and render them useless, they would be extra worried if they went into the women's bathroom. Everyone is so *nice* to each other. It's bananas. In a world where women are ultrasuspicious and ultracritical of other women, there is a respite, in the deep smelly pits of the shittiest places in the world.

Once you enter a woman's bar bathroom line, you are immediately bonded together by the sheer mass of it all. Men's bathroom lines are notoriously empty, only three or four men in a queue, exasperated that they have to wait even five minutes to piss. You can almost hear that entitled-white-dude voice at restaurants and airports: *Why . . . this is . . . this is outrageous!*

To us, three to four others in a line would be a miracle. We would Instagram that shit. We would mark that day in our *calendars.* We are used to "Apple Releasing a New iPhone and Harry Styles Will Kiss You on the Cheek If You Buy It" type of line situations. We just keep clenching and get out our phones.

"Always, always a wait!" the girl in front of me says, a six-foot-two glamazon with a Michael Kors bag and a blowout that spits right in gravity's face. We laugh and smile, knowingly. "Always a wait!" I say to the woman behind me, a model-type who layers her black clothing in inspiring ways. "It's not fair!" she says. And then she compliments my shoes.

The compliments keep on coming as I go up the line. Once I get into the actual restroom, I will be showered with them. "Oh my fucking God, I love your dress! It looks absolutely amazing on you." She is slurring her words, but her eyes do not deceive her. "Oh my God, your skin is perfect!" says one girl to another. A veritable Siren's Chorus emanates from these piss-filled walls, which you practically have to wade through because they are so riddled with loose strands of toilet paper. "Please tell me who does your nails." "Your hair is so frigging beautiful." We are almost ready to jump into the ocean, become mermaids, and start luring sailors to their death. But first, we must trade salon secrets, secrets of Madison Avenue hair artists and Brooklyn manicurists who do reasonably priced nail art.

And oh, the hospitality. If you ever need toilet paper, or tampons, or a lipstick-on-teeth check, this is your place. If you ever need to wash your hands while somebody is in front of you, reapplying perfume, you better believe she steps out of the way. And if you want to cry, cry here. Women you don't know will pet your hair, and tell you that whomever you are crying about is a no-good jerk, even if you are crying about a painful shoe blister. The shoe, in that case, is the jerk! Just throw it out, go to Steve Madden, and try something better! You *deserve it.*

There are only three rules to being accepted in this elusive club: don't throw up, don't try to cut the line (especially with the move Larry David named "the chat and cut"), and don't go into a stall with another friend. Obey, and you will be treated with hospitality unlike you have ever seen.

The moment I leave the bathroom, I snake my way back to the table and into the hellscape, back to reality, whoop there goes gravity. I am side-eyed and elbowed by the very women I just bonded with. We shove past each other and block each other from getting to the bar. We glare at each other if we talk to someone the other is interested in talking to. Some even let their drinks spill just a little onto my dress.

It's time to go home, I think. There's nothing else for me here. I won't have to pee for another twenty minutes (really small bladder) and the subway will take three times as long. I say good-bye all too soon to my real friend, a girl I will no doubt promise brunch tomorrow and cancel on in the morning. But she understands this, because she is my *very good friend*. She and I have spent years cancelling brunch plans, making them again, and finally settling on a movie-and-martini night weeks later. Good friends are the kinds you can cancel on again and again and they will still forgive you.

Making a friend is not a particularly easy task, but it shouldn't be. A good friend is the kind of person whom you will go to the ends of the earth for, even though you think it's kind of fucked up she left your birthday party early. Friends are sometimes better than family, because you can't blame them for your genes, and they are sometimes better than significant others, because you never have to have sex with them when you are tired. I didn't always realize how precious friends, particularly girlfriends, were. For years, I was wary of them. I believed everything I heard about women being friends, which was that being friends with women was horrible and inevitably you get "stabbed" in the back. *Et tu*, Brute?

Once I got over that, I became very enamored of women. There are a lot of uniquely special things about female friendships, and one of them is *how you rank your friends.* Male friendships are mostly classified by "buddy" and "this is another one of my buddies." For women friendships, you can qualify friendships by "many different circles" and "she's my best friend," but you say that for about three different women at any given time, and "oh my God, you are like my sister," which probably means you just met her and are very excited you both like similar things. I will explain this more by letting you know a little bit about my female friends, who are mostly in specific and classified circles:

The smallest circle is a group of four or five women whom I would not go to prison for, but I would *say* that I would go to prison for. These are not my *Sex and the City* women; these are my "dogs in a children's movie who go on a great adventure together." Yes. It is that serious and we are that tightly bound. Some of them I do not really talk to very often, but they have made such a mark on my life that if I ever have children, my children will know who these women are or meet them. I love them dearly. In there is my best friend, Amanda. She is the one I secretly think I could be happily platonically married to, which isn't a secret because I've told her. She has seen me at my worst in a horrifying way—ugly drunk crying, unwashed for days, unaware of 401(k)s or how to zipper up this dress— and at my meanest and most bitter. She is a goddamn treasure. The others are girls I can call or text with very petty worries, mundane life updates, or photos of animals pooping.

Hovering near the first group are two or three women who might eventually enter that inner circle. They are girls I am currently obsessed with and have just started telling all my secrets to. They are the ones I want to see all the time and get drinks with, because we like each other so much. We want to hear all the stories about each other's exes, our confessions about our saddest moments, and stuff about our families we already told our best friends. They will either enter that circle or travel to the next, slightly larger circle of women. Many of them have been hovering for years. They are the ones who will ask me when they read this if they are hovering. The way to enter the inner circle is to be totally fine with me never texting you back. The slightly larger circle of women after that is filled with a handful of women whom I would maybe go to a bridal shower for. They are women I've had real moments with, girls I see all the time and genuinely like. I would go to bat for them as long as I am not too busy, and I have maybe seen them cry once. After that, there is a slightly larger circle whom I like to have at parties I throw, but would never help move. This one changes constantly and will probably get larger with time. Everybody else is just noise.

These circles might sound impressive, but that's because I've been trying and failing at friendships for twenty-six years. The older you get, the harder making friends becomes, and the harder it is to be a good friend, and the harder it is to keep friends.

When I was younger, best friends were easily made and won. I had around ten best friends from the ages of five to twelve. Maybe more. I had best friends for days or years at a time, and acquiring them was as easy as sharing a sandwich or complimenting a lunch box.

There was Dana, the overly Christian girl who won me over with Freeze Pops, a mother who was inclined to buy me both stickers and pretzel Goldfish. We would spend whole mornings creating worlds to the gentle lull of Kathie Lee Gifford and Regis Philbin in the background. She and I had a falling out when her Halloween pumpkin, left on the front porch, was vandalized by a couple of punk teens. I didn't express the proper sympathy, and the damage was irrevocable. There was Ali, who showed me the naughtier side of playing house by spending much of her dollhouse days making Ken and Barbie fornicate, as well as Teresa and Ken, and Ken and Kevin, and Barbie and Teresa and Ken. She would smash them together with such vigor that sometimes their heads would pop off. She told me that sex happened when you ran into each other, naked, at full force. I hope she's learned since, but maybe it is I who is doing it wrong. Our friendship ended when I suggested that maybe the Barbies would like to take a rest from naked wrestling and throw a soiree in the garden. There was Christina, the girl who was shorter than I was who suddenly decided she did not want to be the shortest friend anymore; Nicole, who grew tired of me overindulging on her Arizona Iced Teas; and Katie, who all but threw me into a cubbyhole for the more popular girls.

There was the overzealous "best-friends pact" I made with two girls named Callie, even though they often left me out by going to see *Mulan* without me and having sleepovers they didn't invite me to. I do not believe we were mentally equipped to gracefully maneuver a friendship with an uneven amount of people. Often I would sit by Callie #2's pool, dipping my little feet in and playing the drums on my protruding tummy while the two Callies shared secrets over in a corner somewhere. Being left out is common in friendships with little girls: there was no pushing or shoving, you were either wanted or you weren't. There was whispering, and laughing at inside jokes you didn't know about, and playdates you didn't go to. We were close because we were in the same classes and drifted dutifully apart as we had classes with other people and could make similar best-friends pacts with other girls.

When I got older, there was a confusing hierarchy that came into play with my girlfriends. I had come into alignment with a group of very classic preppy women, the kinds who bought J. Crew that wasn't on sale and didn't even care that J. Crew rarely carried anything in black, usually just NAVY. Two of them really liked me, and the rest thought I was way too loud, which in retrospect was a totally fair assessment of me. Annie was the leader of it all because she smelled like Gap Dream perfume and had enough boyfriends over the years to confirm there was something cool about her. She thought I was wonderful, so the other girls could do nothing but at least pretend to want to give me Bath & Body Works Cucumber Melon lotion when they picked me for Secret Santa. Still, I could barely keep track of where I was in this pyramid of friendship: if I was Annie's third best friend, or her best friend in most of her classes, or her best *best* friend besides Hallie, whom she had known for much longer than me. When I was around them, I felt warmth and comfort. We had sleepovers at Annie's house where we would rewatch the parts in *Harry Potter* where you got a good view of Oliver Wood's butt as he scrambles to catch the Golden Snitch. We would spend hours talking about the same boy I had a crush on since sixth grade, who had the same name as one of the actors in the Brat Pack. My mother thought I was talking about the guy who had starred in *Mannequin* with Kim Cattrall, and not an actual honor student with braces and a penchant for puka shell necklaces.

I also felt cold and rejected at times. The girls who didn't like me whispered behind my back and told rumors about me and went out of their way not to invite me to things. One of them dated the Brat Pack kid, even though she knew I practically had dibs (although he never spoke to me? That's just a formality). I spent a lot of time in high school, and later on in college, feeling rejected by some of the women I knew, and a lot of the time, it was over a guy. In high school, it was because of the Brat Pack. In college, it was because of a pale, awful, boring man, the human equivalent of mayonnaise. I cannot believe the lengths we girls go to compete with each other over guys. Like, don't worry, there will be some other dude who likes pizza for you to go hog wild over. There are millions of these men. Never fight over somebody you want to have sex with, because there will be many more.

There is a catty side to women that I think gets played out a lot in the media, but sometimes, it is very true. Not all women are cruel, and not all are catty, but when you get burned, it sometimes feels like they are. We fight, sometimes, with words and with subtle, icy ways of ignoring people. Glances. Passive-aggressive comments about an outfit. We shoot with invisible arrows that land right in the heart.

It still happens, even as you get older. Just recently, I was at a bar with some girls I knew vaguely. I made a joke and they did that thing where they looked at me like I was an alien and then looked at each other and giggled. I don't have time for this shit! I am a grown-ass woman. But this stuff still happens. I try to ignore it but sometimes, it makes me frustrated. Why? Why be an asshole? Do we have to act like shit to women just to prove the stereotype is true? Isn't it easier just *not* to be an asshole?

It is very easy to think, as a woman, that other women are your competition. I spent much of my life very suspicious of other women, their agendas, and where they might have gotten their shoes. Every time I met one, I assumed she was in

direct competition with me. This could be anything—
competition to be the funniest girl in my group of friends. Or
the prettiest with glasses. Or maybe she was destined to one
day snag the last black sweater, on sale, in a size medium, right
from underneath my desiring paws. Or she would be attractive to the man I am attracted to. Or order the last drip of
Pumpkin Spice at my local coffee shop, even though Pumpkin
Spice is essentially cinnamon flavoring pumped with corn
syrup and is disgusting. I'm not even sure I want half the
things I'm competing for with this new woman I just met and
am suspicious of. Maybe it's her body—she's a size smaller
than I am and looks banging in all the outfits I want to look
good in. Or whatever her size, she's got a "this is my body and
I love it the way it looks" attitude and reminds me how inse-
cure I can be sometimes. Or it's her amazing taste in lipstick
that I can't afford. Or maybe her hair is better, or her job is
more prestigious, or she's one of those girls that have an Etsy
shop. Whatever it is: I can and have found ways to convince
myself she is an enemy of mine.

When women meet other women, there's a reluctance I
don't see with men. Men tend to embrace each other right off
the bat and grow to dislike each other later. They firmly shake
hands. If they meet a friend of a friend, they consider that person a friend. They only grow to despise the person after he tries
to give less money at a group dinner or breaks one of their
glasses or something years later. Me, I've grown up making nice
with the women I am introduced to. I'm friendly with them at
first introduction, these new friends of my good friend, these
new girlfriends. I ask them questions and smile at them. Then,
the next time I see them, I pretty much ignore them, and they
ignore me. We size each other up like opponents. If I see them
twice, it means they are sticking around, and I have to figure

out what they have that I don't. *Then*, after many moons of ignoring them I would happen to sit next to them on a couch and we'd bond over favorite TV shows or sales at Anthropologie or female reproductive rights. I would defrost myself and let them in, just a bit, and suddenly we're saying, "How come we weren't friends earlier?" We know why. We damn well know why.

Still, it doesn't make me change my patterns. There are scores of women I just never defrosted myself with, and I'm just not friends with them. I'm frustrated at how much I have missed out in my youth, my college years, and my early adulthood because I was so wary of other women. And it is a *waste.*

You should never underestimate the power of female friendships. Platonic female relationships, in my mind, are the salted caramel or the truffle salt of the relationship world. They provide you a specific kind of love that is unparalleled. It's domestic in its content. It can be years of bliss, without worry that your friend will leave, without fear that she will let you down. It is the stuff that pop singers write ballads about, truly.

It's hours of lying on couches and watching TV together, picking at your toenails or popping pimples or putting creams on your faces. You take off your makeup and talk about zits and eat entire bags of chips and pints of ice cream till you're both so gassy you might explode. It is hours of honest conversation, telling each other the raw soul and essence of yourself—every fear, every pregnancy scare, every sexual inclination, every feeling about what the future holds.

You cycle up your periods if you both get them. You share clothing and give each other honest opinions on what looks good and what doesn't, on your breasts and stomachs. You try new things together like bikini waxes and palm readings, but it's not all surface shit. You grow together, and you see each other fail and succeed. You encourage exploration. You tell each other your desires and the things you are scared to tell other people. You can get into petty little arguments and snip at each other because you're not worried that you won't be friends forever. You get so angry at each other when the other person doesn't see how beautiful she is. You get angry at each other when the other settles for less. You get dressed up and meet for cocktails and fancy, expensive dinners, or treat each other with extravagant birthday gifts that are so catered to the other person's tastes, it's as if she chose it herself.

I understand that of course there's a screening process to this kind of intimate, special relationship. It takes time to develop, and is rare. Not every woman-on-woman friendship is going to be as beautiful. But even casual female friendships can be very rewarding.

Having a group of female friends you enjoy is very important so you can meet up for wine-bender "Girls' Nights." You go savage animal on wine and drink bottles and bottles of it. Usually you start off at some Francophile's wet dream realized into a shitty bar with wine bottles for half off and a cheese plate. You swoop in and destroy the place, like giant birds of prey. Bottles are consumed at a frantic rate, as if wine somehow won't exist anymore unless you fill your entire body with it. The more you drink, the more you insert raunchy sex jokes into the conversation and, eventually, talk about anal sex and why you would/wouldn't do it. Then you go to another bar (one without FOOD, no less), even though you hate bars, to get your single friend laid, and you're too happy from the wine to complain about it. So you just sort of jauntily grunt at whatever person your single friend is into and are unable to gracefully transition into vodka sodas. Then you go home and you text each other dancing lady emojis while drunkenly eating stale bread. The only consequence of all this is liver problems and that your friend might ask you to be her bridesmaid at a destination wedding somewhere you've never wanted to visit.

Casual female friends are also useful for shopping trips and happy hours and for dinners where you get to talk about your entire life and then hear opinions about your entire life. You just talk about yourself, which is wonderful, and they listen. Then, you talk about going to a spin class together or one of those pottery classes where you can drink wine. You never do this. The only consequence of this is that she may tell your other mutual close friends about your shitty life choices.

Recently, in my older and wiser years, I have tried to make an abundance of female friends. Like I said, this is difficult and I'm not quite sure how to go about it in the right way. Without the structure of school, it's hard to meet people organically, but it's also hard to meet people in general. I don't want to be too pushy. I don't know how to approach females with my guard down, kind of like, "Hey, I'm over being kind of rude and indifferent to other women, let's grab lunch!" It's hard. It feels unnatural. I don't have the foundation or the practice to be good at making friends with women, because I've spent years of my life being defensive with the ones I do not know. Whenever a female is nice to me, I want to shake her and say, "Who are you working for! *Who sent you?!*" I am *still* afraid of other women, quite frankly. I am afraid that they will not accept me, or that they will be petty and mean to me, even though I don't play that game anymore. It is hard to ignore behaviors I have seen before and not react the way I usually do.

It's not easy. But it can be done. You might still get burned, of course, but odds are that you won't.

Three particular female friendships I made later in life happened when I did in fact put myself out there. One woman e-mailed me out of the blue and asked me to dinner. One was an ex-fling of a good friend. And one was one of my best friend's childhood friends. Each friendship took some time to develop. Our relationships were shaky, and I approached them in an almost catlike way. I nuzzled up to these women slowly, offering little bits of information about myself like kibble. I pushed myself to be friendly. It felt uncomfortable, almost like I was dating again, and I had to make an overabundance of small talk I'd rather not have made. I told them who I was. I didn't come at them with a sense of "you're beautiful and I am intimidated," even though they were beautiful and I was intimidated. I got dinner with them. I kept promises and plans. And slowly, slowly, they became my friends. My partners in wine crime and advisers on statement necklaces. It is work, but it is important work.

Having women as allies and not looking at them as enemies is so crucial to your development as a woman. To love women not in spirit but in practice: to be kind, generous, and open to them and see which ones stick. To come at other women with a white flag of friendship, and be prepared that they might not be in the same mind-set, and to take that rejection in stride and not let it hurt you. I want to try to make friends with women because it is ultimately very rewarding to me. Women are fantastic. They are beautiful allies to have, not enemies. Some are assholes, just like many people are, but you can find the good ones if you have your eyes open, and develop a community of people around you who have your back. It's a wonderful feeling. My advice? Try to be like Selma Blair and Reese Witherspoon at the end of *Legally Blonde*: ditch the competition and become friends instead. There will be another guy who texts winky faces at all hours of the night in no time, and you can both get the things you want out of life.

Even if you don't want to be friends: start off nice, continue to be courteous and kind, and let the weight of competition, of wariness, fall from your shoulders. It is a burden just waiting to be lifted.

With this in mind, I've also learned what it takes to be a good friend. Admitting I wasn't always the best at it, that sometimes the way people acted toward me negatively was also a result of me acting negatively toward them, wasn't easy. But man, you have to learn:

To be a good friend, you have to keep in touch. You have to send your friends notes that you are thinking of them, even if you are busy, even if you have a new boyfriend or girlfriend you want to kiss, even if you just send quick texts. You have to listen and remember things about them. You have to let their problems trump your own sometimes, even if you are frustrated with your own life. You have to let them eat your French fries, even if they didn't order them because they are on a diet.

Let them borrow the clothes they want, but you do not have to let them borrow your makeup or your most expensive jewelry. Tell them what looks good on them, and what doesn't. Be honest with them about 99 percent of the time, but use a bit of honey when you are feeding them vinegar. Let them talk to you about the same problems a million times. Know their favorite foods and be prepared to bring those foods over when they are sick or in mourning. Be there. Use caution when criticizing their significant others, but never stand silent and watch them get hurt. Let them know when they are too drunk or too angry or being unfair. Let them know when they get stagnant. Give them unsolicited advice. Give them love. Give them good presents. Talk shit when necessary. Listen. Help them pick out a haircut. Tell them they are pretty. Tell them they are smart. Tell them how to ask for a raise at work. Set aside whole days for them. *BE THERE*. And don't break plans . . . twice in a row.

I've also learned what it takes to be a good person to other women, in general, even if you aren't sure you will be their friend:

Smile. Say hi. Give them compliments whenever they look good. Seriously. Compliments go a long way. Ask them questions. Remember their names. Be friendly first. Be open. Take it from there.

Being a friend or an ally to other women is both difficult and rewarding. I still don't think I have it all down. However— the easiest way to begin?

Treat women like you just met them in a bar bathroom. You just never know what could become of it.

I Am Exactly like Other Girls

Before I was a feminist, I was an asshole.

Assholes don't always know they are being assholes. Assholes who don't know they are assholes are the kind of people who tell you about fights they've started in grocery stores, expecting you to think it wasn't their fault. They'll get angry with waiters for being slow and expect you to back them up. They'll take phone calls wherever they feel like it because they think they have the most important ones. For me, I was an asshole because I did not understand I was an asshole to other women.

When I was in college, I would have told you at the time that I was a very big ally to other women. I thought that being a very big ally to other women only meant that you (a) were a woman, (b) weren't as mean to women as other women were, and (c) were definitely not as mean to women as men were. I wouldn't have called myself *a feminist*, or anything. No, no, *no*. I wasn't a feminist, because I had a sense of humor. I wasn't a feminist, because I liked men too much. I wasn't a feminist, because if you work hard enough, you can get anything that men have. I wasn't a feminist, because I wasn't a lesbian. I wasn't a feminist, because I needed to learn, but of course I didn't know that yet.

Women were fine, but I had this horrible affliction of being *nothing* like them. We didn't get along. I got along with my friends, of course, but they weren't like other women. I was desperately afraid of being associated with all the stereotypical and awful traits that women got saddled with. So this made me different. *I wasn't like other women.* Cool as a cucumber. Chill like ice. So chill, I was almost like a man in the way that I was very chill. I really wasn't like *regular* girls. Regular girls were all the bad things men said about women: difficult and dramatic. Guys were *easier*, I said, and I was hoping "by association" would get me a few cool points in all the basements of all the men I hung out with. So I lived my life feeling better and very different, even though no matter how you look at it, there are no separate categories for "cool woman" and "regular woman." There are just women.

Nobody is born a feminist. As much as I like to think the world will one day be swimming with babies wearing pro-choice pins on rompers of their own volition, it just isn't so. And as much as I like to think I will one day have a daughter who will be born knowing she can do absolutely anything in the whole world that a man can do, it's something I'll have to teach her. And as much as I like to think that little boys will stop pushing the little girls they have crushes on . . . oh wait, we actually have to stop teaching them that shitty behavior, too.

Becoming a feminist, unfortunately, sometimes means having some bad experiences that make you realize the importance of it all. There are only so many times you can be cat-called, hear and experience sexism, be groped at parties, and called a slut before you start questioning the world around you. It also takes a willingness to call yourself a feminist because many people will think you're a radical nut job. And you have to be *real* willing to be okay with that. As somebody who usually likes to be liked, I found this situation difficult to overcome.

I look at the time between ages seventeen and twenty-one as my pre-feminism years with both fascination and mild disgust, emotions usually reserved for watching eating competitions on television. When I reflect back, I just want to sit down and shake myself. I have wasted so much of my life caring more about being cool than about giving myself and other women a shot. I have wasted so much time being an asshole just to be accepted.

To be honest, I look back at most of my life and cringe at *many* of my life decisions that came from a place of "accept me." Some of these aren't super harmful. For instance, there's a school picture in which I wore a metal headband with butterflies that changed color in the sun. I've pretended to see and like a million different movies and television shows just so people will shut up about me not having seen them. I've bought polo shirts and denim skirts and graphic T-shirts that were just the style in high school even though I wanted to cough blood onto them. I've gone on dates just so I could tell friends I was dating. I've joined a Fantasy Football League. I've had oysters because I wanted to feel French even though it felt like I was swallowing a lougie. I've had bangs and expensive unlimited booze brunches and one more drink and maybe just a hit and okay, *I guess I can go upstairs with you*. So I know what it's like to do things because I want to fit in.

There are also plenty of things I've done to be accepted that are downright tacky. I imagine you know what I'm talking about. The silence when somebody's talking badly about a friend of yours. The laughter at a shitty offensive joke. Leaving people out because somebody doesn't like them. Calling some-body fat or a whore. "Fitting in" is one of those horrible dis-eases that turn reasonable minds into sheep-gelatin hive minds.

When I look back on it, I think I spent a lot of my young adulthood trying to make certain people like me and certain men love me. That was sort of my calling card. "Alida Nugent: Granter of Men's Wishes." Instead of a lamp, you could have put me in some sort of bong, I bet.

I wasn't a particularly interesting person when I was try-ing to fulfill these wishes. I know that I was a vibrant and funny girl when I was alone with my friends. With friends, I was brassy in the kind of way that Fran Drescher was in *The Nanny*, all "who cares about eating this pizza, honey, check out the gams on that dude, wooo give me some vodka" and large accessories and big hair. I also know that inside, I wasn't so vibrant—trying to be the thinnest I could be, the prettiest, the most willing, and the one every guy thought was . . .

Ugh. You guessed it. *Cool.* Fuck cool, man. I hate being cool now. I'm not cool, and I'm totally fine with that. I don't want to be the kind of girl who rolls her eyes and tries her dandiest to emulate Rizzo, who was cool because she was *genuinely cool.* There are plenty of women and people who are genuinely cool. I think Angelina Jolie is cool. I think Julianne Moore and Ju-liette Lewis and Eartha Kitt and Anjelica Huston and Cather-ine Keener are cool because they don't try; they're just naturally allergic to bullshit and their voices are raspy. Most people are not cool. *Trying* to be cool is overrated and downright boring. I'm so tired of everybody talking about how enthusiasm is stu-pid, as if wearing leather jackets and using the phrase "I hate people" is something that makes you interesting.

I was that girl, though, back in the day. I tried to roll cigarettes and ended up getting tobacco in every corner of my house. My strategy for meeting men at parties was to go up to the grodiest, angriest-looking one and start talking about how everybody was shit, the world was shit, and all I cared about was art. I think my main goal was to become the kind of girl written into misogynist literature. Not even the literature the world actually thinks is good. I'm talking about some scraggly dude's piece-of-shit MFA story he wrote because he hated high school and he had that stupid Hunter S. Thompson poster in his room to inspire him. In it, "the protagonist," aka him, meets a nice prostitute, a beautiful prostitute, and it changes him. Or he meets an angry, tortured woman, and she gets to serve as the kind of woman who moves the narrative along by being aggressive and by helping a man reach the lesson of the story. *That* kind of girl. I was there to nod, and show my tits just a little, and try to be a guy's girl while wearing a short skirt. I was there to say that I hated parties, too, and to admire the fact that he drank whiskey, neat, not even on the rocks or anything. *Oh, wow, super cool, you don't use water in solid form, let me rip off my clothes now! How is your relationship with your mother, by the way? Oh, you think she's the only woman you'll ever love? Let me shovel my underwear into a fire pit, I don't need it anymore!*

The first thing you do as a girl trying to be cool is betray women everywhere. Okay, okay, the first thing *I did* was watch *Fight Club*, read *Fight Club*, and then talk about how awesome the movie and the book both were, as well as the differences between the two, to the guys I was hoping to impress. Then, I betrayed women everywhere. No—no, then I found somebody to have a crush on who wears hats indoors. Then, I gently threw women under the bus. Like I said, I wasn't like other women! I threw them under buses and read popular books-turned-movies with Brad Pitt!

To me, it didn't *feel* like betrayal. Like I said, I was totally cool with women. I just didn't need to be seen or associated with them. I was a tomboy, a guy's girl, the scrappy token female in the gang who always says, "Let me at 'em, boss!" but they won't let her fight because she's a chick. The only thing worse, by the way, than trying to be cool all the time is declaring yourself a "guy's girl." And that's just who I was, man.

Ah, to be the kind of person who declares that she *just doesn't get along with that many women.* What this can also be translated to is, "I don't get along with *half the entire world.*" This is not a "them problem." This is most definitely a "you problem." Women who say they do not get along with other women have a laundry list of reasons why this is so, and all of them are stupid (misguided). The most common reason is because they find girls to be catty. They find them to be mean to them because they are jealous. And! They just. Don't. Like. The. DRAMA! I'm not talking about Shakespeare, of course. I'm talking about the tragedy and comedy of girls who all hang out together and subsequently invite to, disinvite to, and fight each other at various Solo Cup parties.

I'm not going to say that women don't do those things. They do, because they have been encouraged to fight with words rather than fists. Women, by and large, are certainly encouraged to use their words more than men, and it results in womenfolk airing their grievances both in front of women and behind their backs. I've never quite been able to dissect what constitutes drama and what doesn't, but it usually centers around people women want to have sex with, parties, and things people may or may not have said. And, here is all I'm saying—as much drama as you receive, you deliver. I've seen *The Hills.*

Women are pitted against each other all the damn time. In

my eyes, we're stumbling over each other, tripping each other to prove that we're the dream girl you've always wanted to meet. The one woman who is not like women at all. I'm not gonna get all prissy when you ask me to go camping. I know what football is. I eat hamburgers with both my hands, not like those other girls who have to diet to be skinny. I'm easygoing with whatever you want to do at the moment. I'm beautiful, I'm gorgeous, I'm put together, but you'll never see how I'm put together. You'll just see sexy ole me, eating chicken wings with a flat stomach, totally content to hang with all the boys.

I idolized the importance of men in such a way that I thought the closer I was to them, the more they would like and accept me, and the more I emulated them, the better I would be for it. I understood that men had a place of power in the world, and I was one ambitious little lady. Ambitious girls, before they found feminism, used to think they had to act like men to get ahead in the world. You're not a friend to women, or an ally to women, if you think that in general women aren't as good, as ambitious, or as powerful as men.

The worst part about my pre-feminism days, and those years before I came to realize the importance of feminism, was the shameful things I did with my words. So often, we fight with our words and do not realize the impact of them. In college, I became particularly fond of the word "slut." I didn't use it flippantly; I thought it held real power when appropriate. The reason I liked the word "slut" was because it could differentiate "other women" from those women I liked. A slut was anybody who had sex with numerous men, and I used the word in front of a group of friends I wanted to like me. A slut was any girl who had sex with somebody I wanted to have sex with, because if I were looser he would probably have had sex with me.

I didn't realize that calling a girl a slut because she slept with somebody, or more than one person, or wore low-cut tops made it all the easier to judge me when I did those things. It made it okay for the word to be directed at me. It established that having consensual sex *could* be used to judge somebody. Using the word "slut" was a real mudsling, except the mud usually ended up on me, too. There were plenty of different words I used with the sole purpose of sliding other women down a peg and pushing me up one.

Like "crazy." Any girl was crazy because she expressed her opinions or called people out. How deeply and enthusiastically I nodded when a guy called another woman crazy, particularly his ex-girlfriends. How quickly we use that word, even though I myself have an anxiety disorder and frequent panic attacks and a brain that, on occasion, severely dislikes me. How easily it stigmatizes those who suffer from mental disorders, or even those who are just *expressive*. How often I fight to not feel crazy, and yet how quickly I doled it out to others. I've *been* the crazy one. I've been the crazy girl who called the guy again to find out why he had stopped talking to me. I've been the crazy girl who went to the party to try to be visible to somebody who didn't notice me. I never realized how often it would come right back to me, how dismissive people could be toward women whenever they were telling the truth, loudly.

There are other words, too. Bossy. Bitchy. Rude. Fat. Ugly. Stupid. Whore. I used these words when I had an agenda. I was always looking for ways to frame other women in a way that made me *seem better* and more appealing. *I* was the cool girl, not her, don't you see? Every time I used these phrases, these cheap shots, it was just so I could seem *less* like those words. She's uglier than I am. She's a real bitch. She slept with more people.

It's pointing out these cardinal sins so I won't get blamed for them. How many fucking times did I sit around with guys hearing "yeah, you're not like *that* kind of girl" and feel absolute victory? I knew somebody would be the whore. It just never occurred to me that maybe *nobody* had to be.

When I was an asshole, my relationship to other women was "it's not me, it's *her.*" It was finger-pointing. It was "look over there." And eventually, I would gain an audience for it.

In college, I decided to try my hand at stand-up comedy. In one of my very first classes, an introduction to screenwriting, you had to do a monologue, and a guy who did comedy in the local bars saw it. He said I should try it out and he could take me to an open mic. I think he said this because he had a crush on me, and he thought it would be a nice thing to say, and also I was one of those girls who didn't get nervous speaking in public. I said I'd do it, and I did it pretty consistently for three years.

Being a woman in comedy is hard. Just as being in any male-dominated field is hard. If you like comics, sci-fi, music, science, technology, or video games, you know what I'm talking about. There's a male possessiveness over these things, guarded by "the big boys" who think they own the joint, and you should feel lucky if you're even allowed to step inside. Then, when they *let* you step inside, they deny there's ever a problem. Then they ogle your breasts. Then they tell you you're nuts for even thinking there's a problem! It's gaslighting by the kind of men who turned to these venues for some sense of camaraderie, then get all choosy about who gets to come into the club.

In my experience with comedy, I had to think about being a woman almost constantly. When you are a female comedian, there's a big sign over your head that says LADY and TALK

ABOUT YOUR TITS and TELL US WHO YOU HAVE SEX WITH. When
you start, you are the lady at the very bottom of a small mountain, a mountain covered with the kind of men who have neck-
beards. You do what you can to survive, and almost all of it is
difficult and slightly untrue to yourself. I never felt so small
and I never felt the need to be so *loud*.

If you are a woman in comedy, chances are you've said
something you didn't really believe in, something you didn't
really even want to *say*, because you were trying to be the funniest woman in the room. When you are a chick, you can't call
yourself a comic without saying, "I am a woman comic." The
two are intertwined so tightly, said with the kind of sarcasm
and venom that says, "Eh, you can be here, but you'll never
really belong."

Now, of course, there are plenty of female comedians who
stay true to themselves and don't go straight to shock comedy
and women bashing. I have to believe these women have some
sort of emotional security and confidence and foresight. But I
was nineteen and already plenty misguided and had none of
those qualities, so it was enough for me to go headfirst in that
negative direction.

At first, my comedy was centered around shock—just your
typical comments about sex and periods and how I used a vibrator sometimes. It's sort of like pratfalls on television: they're
the cheapest, quickest way to get a laugh. I caught on to this
pretty quickly, specifically because I was performing around
drunk people. If you say "sex" to a crowd of drunk people,
they tend to laugh immediately. The ironic part was that I
wasn't even having sex. There are great female comics who
talk about sex because they are trying to change the way sex is
discussed, or because they genuinely enjoy it. *I*, however, was
knee-deep into feeling pretty bad about a guy I was seeing

who didn't even live in the same city as I did. I didn't have sex at all. I made out with people at parties, sometimes. But I could still cobble together a couple of sex anecdotes that hid all the parts about me that I didn't want the audience to see, like my emotional frailness and whatnot. There was nothing genuine about my dirty talk. But hey! People laughed. Or men laughed, I should say.

The first time I did an open mic in a club, nobody thought I was going to be funny. Around the fiftieth time, I found that people still thought I wasn't going to be funny. And whenever I got laughs, I felt pretty good about myself, but never felt like I was progressing any more from the last time. The open mic hosts would always introduce you as "a funny little lady" or "this next lady" instead of "this next comic." I would head into open mics and sit in the very back, inching myself next to the only other woman who was there, looking at her for some kind of sage guidance. Instead, she spent most of the time playing and goofing with the guys.

Every time I would show up to a club, somebody would ask me whose girlfriend I was. That, to me, is incredible. It's not like NO WOMAN has ever done comedy ever. It's not like there is no evidence that women also go up to the mic and perform comedy, or that they can't speak. We are not all post-leg Ariels, putting forks in our hair and being generally confused about the human world. But like clockwork, somebody would ask whose girlfriend I was, and I would say, "No one's. It's just me," and then go up there and do a five-minute set about sex during menstruation.

Sometime in the second year I decided I would be the best comic that I could be, which meant being even louder and raunchier than I was before. I also decided that I would use my greatest disadvantage (being a woman) to my greatest advantage (making fun of it constantly). It's like riding in on the elephant in the room, but everybody talks about the elephant and knows it is there. So I centered my comedy around all the things that being a woman meant and tried to make it my shtick. You know, typical harmless stuff about how my breasts are big, and women are always worried about one-night stands, and tampon bits. I went around town talking *at* men about women, like somehow we all had the same views and I was just sort of the spokesperson for them, on account of me being the only chick there.

There's also always a question in any comic's mind about how much a comic can push the limit. It happens when you start getting comfortable onstage with your material, when you think you have an audience of people on your side and you can make your mark. People will, generally, remember you if you're offensive. The thing about these offensive jokes is, 50 percent of the time, the comic is absolutely thinking she is making a *statement*. She thinks she is making political commentary that will go down in history as something meaningful. The people who see past the offensiveness will understand this! Simply acknowledging that a thing exists is commentary in people's minds. A comic makes a joke about the Holocaust? Ha! She's reminding you the Holocaust existed! She makes a joke about race? She's simply reminding you that people are racists! Since I was capitalizing on women, I made a joke about assault. The ignorance I displayed, and the utter shame I feel about it now, are reasons I am a feminist today.

The particular joke I made (which is still on the Internet! Hooray!) was about babies birthed from campus assault. I said that when explaining how one of these babies was born, the mother would have to say that she was walking home late at night in a short skirt and that her grandparents were Catholic, so she had to have the kid.

This to me was boundary-pushing commentary. A *woman?! Acknowledging these things that are real, horrible problems?!* I thought it was framed in a way that all the viewers who heard it would understand I thought it was simply *nuts* that people get attacked for short skirts and that religion policed women's bodies. I was aware that these were problems, and I thought because they *could* happen to me, I was allowed to make a joke about them. Maybe I can. Maybe I can make all the tasteless jokes about assault I want, but that doesn't mean they're funny.

And here is what I remember. The joke landed, but it landed for the wrong reasons. It came across that assault was okay, at the very least an all-right punch line. If there was a man in that audience who kissed somebody when she didn't want him to, if there was a man there who got a girl home with him when she was too drunk to say no, I made that man feel okay. If there was a girl in that audience who was one of the five estimated to be assaulted on a college campus today, I didn't make her feel empowered. I made her feel like a victim, again. I made her feel like a joke.

Stand-up never fulfilled me the way I thought it would. I wish it were because I realized the spinelessness of some of my jokes, but that came later. Nope. I didn't like being a stand-up comedian because I didn't like how it felt to be a woman in a room full of men. I had to face being a girl, not a *cool girl* who knew all the tricks, but a girl just like any other girl, and guess what? I didn't fucking like it. I wasn't smart enough to change yet. I wasn't strong enough to deal with it. And I wasn't self-aware enough to use it to my advantage. But a tiny, tiny seed was planted, and I finally began to learn. It took me a long time to find my voice, with help from the Internet and by attending a liberal arts college and getting a little more mature. I found my voice, eventually, when I started writing what I knew.

I knew a little about being a woman, both the good things and the bad things about it. I found that writing comedy directed toward ladies was more interesting and exciting than just writing comedy explaining women to men. I began to write solely for women and about women. I started writing satires about women's magazines, comedy write-ups about shows like the *The Bachelorette*, *Sex and the City*, and other things that elicited an "oh God, I know!" from the ladies in my life. I began to take a greater joy in talking about women (with other women, no less) than I had taken joy in anything else in my life. It wasn't about comparison, or cool points. I began to write from a place not of fear or self-consciousness, but pure joy. I didn't know that it would be the start to the women-centric blog that would eventually get me my book deal, but hey. Life is weird, and sometimes you get to pay for your mistakes, and sometimes you get to realize them, and sometimes you get to redeem yourself a little bit.

People always ask me how I knew I was a feminist. There was no aha moment. I simply made a bunch of mistakes. Then, after a long time, I realized them, and finally stopped hating myself, and started *liking* being a woman.

Around my senior year of college, I took a stand-up class once more. I had to do one set at the end of the year, which to date is the last time I've ever done stand-up.

I made a joke about a popular women's magazine. It had published an article about how women often are assaulted because they don't say no loudly enough. I'm not kidding. I read the title out loud and ended my set with: "Ah, women's magazines. Pushing women forward by making assault *sort of their fault."* It might not have been the perfect joke, but I was proud of it. I was finally learning who I wanted to be—not one of the guys, not the lady comic, not the cool girl. Me.

And I was turning out to be a fighter.

I needed feminism at nineteen more than I knew. I wish I had learned sooner that I needed it. All the things I thought about it were wrong. When I became a feminist, I no longer wanted to be cool. I embraced the feminine sides I was afraid of before—I love wearing dresses, and makeup, and cooking because I *love those things*, not because I think I have to. I also thought more about what I said and how it affected the world around me. I related to the world as a woman in the world, instead of trying to catch up with the big boys. The world is still dominated by men, but I'm not trying to be like them anymore. That feels pretty damn good.

My advice to you is to be the feminist that I couldn't be. Immerse yourself in the idea that you can be your own best advocate. Unlearn harmful behaviors. Teach yourself, be active, *embrace* it.

To be a feminist, to believe in equality, to protect yourself and all the women you know, you need to actively think about women. You don't get to shortchange them by calling yourself a humanist. You don't get to disassociate from the word. You don't get to occasionally make stupid jokes because you don't consider yourself accountable for them. You don't get to call a girl a slut because you feel bad about yourself. You need to be an example so others won't have to go through the adolescence we did: trying to fit into a boy's club, or trying to be the kind of girl you thought you *had* to be. You need to embrace the word "feminist" in all its difficulty. You need to take responsibility for it. This is why it is imperative to declare yourself a feminist, to take hold of the word and make it acceptable so younger women can declare it. You need to help women by helping yourself.

I wasn't born a feminist, but I wasn't born an asshole, either. I chose to be both. And boy, have I been both. So call this an official apology. Call it repentance. Fuck, call it covering my bases if you want to. I'm telling you the dirty truth because I want you to know that you can *grow* into a feminist. You can make mistakes; you can have missteps; you can be a downright self-hating woman and still grow to learn and grow to change. But you need to try. You need to start calling yourself a feminist so we can grow together.

I want you to be a flawed feminist, and an imperfect one.

Just like any other girl.

Shrink

When I made the decision to throw up my food for the very first time, it wasn't a spur-of-the-moment kind of thing. The whole awful ordeal began with reasoning, preparation, curiosity, and desperation, like how one might plan a much-needed vacation. When you're nerdy and sixteen as I was, you don't just throw up your food without putting some thought into it first. And for a girl like me—smart, anxious, a perfectionist, unable to please herself, never feeling like she could please others, troubled, and just sad—I needed a vacation from my own brain. I vouched for a quick fix, instead. A release that would momentarily solve my problems while creating even bigger, even more dangerous ones.

But before I jumped into my eating disorder, I needed to do my research. I used to volunteer at a library early in high school, and I was in charge of organizing the YA fiction section. Instead of organizing, I mostly just sat in a corner and read all the books that were about nice girls writing in their diaries about tragic things.

Books about teenagers often portray kids' lives as more traumatic than they are in real life. I read a lot about teenagers joining cults, despite having never met a teenager who had joined a cult. I read about teenagers getting cancer and falling in love with other teenagers getting cancer, in a series of books by Lurlene McDaniel. I read about teenagers having sex and getting pregnant and then *dying*. I read at least three or four books in which somebody had sex and then died. At least half the YA books I read had somebody die. All of them had teenagers who came from horrible homes—sometimes the homes were horrible in the way that featured a brassy mother who smoked cigarettes and left the Malibu just *lying* around the house; sometimes they were just horrible because the parents were psychiatrists and thought that children should spend a lot of time with their parents. Either way, horrible. The girls fell in love with boys with reputations and leather jackets. The girls' whole romantic blossoming took place on the wrong side of the tracks. I spent 240 pages with them as they grew up and lost their innocence and sometimes their lives, and then I closed the book and stopped thinking about them.

The stories about girls with eating disorders, however, were the ones that stuck with me. These girls often came from rich suburban households. They had mothers who loved them. They had futures ahead of them, which explained this incessant need for perfectionism they often had in regard to their bodies. I related to them in some ways. I related to them because I was a normal girl who grew up in a middle-class suburb with nothing real to complain about, yet, I just couldn't stop hating myself. No matter how good my circumstances were, no matter how much my parents supported me, no matter how much food and shelter I had, I couldn't get rid of that hate. It was like a heavy chain around my neck, and I was just worried that one day I would fall into a lake and drown in it.

The books weren't the catalyst for my eating disorder.

They just fueled me. Anybody with an eating disorder will tell you that the catalyst for it is always, always the person herself. Nobody could dredge up more cruelty, more uncertainty, or send more dislike my way than I could. I was the fire. I also lit the match that started it.

Ever since I could weigh myself, ever since I could look at myself in the mirror with a critical eye, I have wanted the Perfect Body. I was obsessed with the idea of it, convinced that my body was not adequate. I saw myself as lumpy and disproportionate. I knew that I had some good parts, although none of them were physical attributes. I knew I was funny, I knew that I was great at English class, and I was helpful and good with adults. But none of it mattered, because I knew how important appearances were, and I knew that I didn't have a perfect body, and I knew how important that was in the world. I wanted that body instead. If only I could figure out what that body was.

The Perfect Body was impossible to achieve but imperative to have. It changed all the time, depending on whom you talked to. What movies you liked. What you were currently reading. What famous women you found to be beautiful. Whether it was a Monday or a Tuesday, practically.

The Perfect Body was always taller than my four-foot-eleven frame. Maybe it was bronzed skin, if I was looking at swimsuit models that week. My skin was yellowish and had nowhere near a glow. Sometimes the Perfect Body was ghostly pale, almost delicate like lace. It was big breasts: real-looking, perky big breasts that had no stretch marks and sat in the middle of the chest, equidistant. I liked the look of small breasts, too. If I had small breasts I could wear thin bras and fashionable clothing. The Perfect Body was a flat stomach. Sometimes I liked the look of ribs poking out; sometimes I liked ab definition. Sometimes I liked the look of those too-cool stoner girls who lived cheaply and always ate Takis from the corner store, or the look of a girl in a bleak independent movie. Sometimes the Perfect Body was a tiny waist with perfect, hourglass curves. Sometimes it would be stick thin, sometimes more athletic, sometimes curvier. I had gone through puberty and got stretch marks. I had a short torso. I was round in all the wrong places and flat in others. I wasn't like any of the women I thought looked like what people liked to see. I never saw me, anywhere. All I saw was what I didn't look like.

There are girls who want a great body, and there are girls who try to get the Perfect Body. The girls who are lost are the ones striving for perfection. Deep down, they know it doesn't exist, but it doesn't stop them from trying.

You can't always tell who they are. Sometimes, the lost girls are like Liv Tyler in *Empire Records*, skinny already with smooth hair and heavy expectations. They are on the honor roll but in the way that they always have to talk about how much they are studying, and it's never enough. They put too much worry into what their parents think about them. They don't get in trouble. They have put so much pressure on themselves you think they're bound to explode. They are the tightly wound rubber band girls, trying so hard to please.

Sometimes, they're the wild ones. They drink too much peach schnapps in their parents' basement. They're damn well convinced the entire world is against them, and they're almost right. They smoke as many cigarettes as they can find and wear rings on all their fingers and are a very bad influence on very good girls. They wear ripped tights and meet boys on the corner and go to graveyards to drink and get fucked. They are a lesson, a lesson to be learned. A lesson that you can't be too wild or too fast.

Sometimes, the lost girls are just sad. They think they're bound to die young. They listen to Joni Mitchell songs on old records and have the kind of long hair that you can do fishtails and medieval braids with. They are always melancholy from loving too much, and they're almost always cold. They are best wrapped in blankets, held by wrists with blue veins. They are best in the rain, in fields where they can put flowers in their hair like they are at their own makeshift funerals.

Or they are girls like me, chubby with braces and no friends. I was loud and clumsy, but I wanted to be mysterious, tortured. My problems were exactly what the #firstworldproblems hashtag refers to, but because I was a teenager and teenagers are hurting, it was not as funny. I lived in a big house with loving parents who, at my heaviest and my thinnest, told me I was the most beautiful girl in the world. It would never be their fault. I was one of those lost girls. I wanted so desperately to be saved. I never got saved. I would get a T-shirt printed if I could:

I WAS BULIMIC AND ALL I GOT WAS A SORE THROAT.

Yeah. Maybe people don't write stories about the tiny buck-toothed girl with bulimia and a horribly pastel Aeropostale wardrobe, but that's me. I guess I'll have to tell my own story.

The truth was, it didn't matter what kind of girl I was, because it happens to so many different girls. My story isn't unique: I had bulimia and then I didn't have it. You wouldn't know I had it unless I told you I did. I'm better now, arguably really good now. But at one point, I wasn't good at all. It was just a facet of my life, a circumstance of being a girl who didn't like herself. But it's common, and it happens often. I was a statistic. A girl in a sea of girls who hated herself so much, she decided to do something about it.

I had bulimia from late high school to mid-college. I call it an illness rather than a disease, because I inflicted it on myself but I wasn't mentally sound enough to act any other way. It was a devastating illness nonetheless, one that came from a cocktail of youthful issues: the need to structure something in my life, my incredible lack of self-esteem, my belief that looking thin was more important than anything in the world, my desire to shrivel up and practically disappear, my desire to be sick because I felt sick and crazy and unstable. It was bad.

The thing I remember most vividly about bulimia was how many rules I had to follow because of it. As a nerdy girl with a Hermione Granger–sized fear of getting in trouble without all the "we still do it anyway" attitude of Hermione Granger, I loved rules. I thrived on them. Ever since I was a kid, I took school and authority seriously. It was just one of my things—I was a type A personality who liked knowing what I could and could not do. But damn, did I secretly want to be rebellious. I wanted, so badly, to be a bad girl. This made bulimia my rebellion of choice. I could be bad, in my own home, and still have enough rules to feel comfortable about the whole thing. There was a certain structure that came along with having this illness, restrictions that kept me on pace and on track.

For instance: I couldn't eat at restaurants without a private bathroom stall. I couldn't go to sleepovers. I couldn't survive without a hair tie around my wrist to hold my hair back. I couldn't flush once. I had to do it quick, without anyone noticing. In an odd silver lining, I also had to be thorough at cleaning toilets, which is a skill that has proved quite useful in my healthier years. But I also couldn't be left alone with a fridge full of cream cheese and no supervision. And I absolutely couldn't wear lip gloss. I never knew if I would eat too many

Cheetos that day and have to take a quick pop into the loo to barf it all out. It was graphic, but also, like the seventeen-year-old honor roll student I used to be, reeked of practicality.

In hindsight, I know that high school is a festering pit of boredom and hormones, not to be taken as seriously as it seemed while I was there. It is earthly purgatory before you enter the better parts of your life: you've got one foot in heaven and the other in hell. Heaven is getting into cars with your friends without parental supervision, the joys of dry humping, and the excitement of going to a diner for pancakes at one a.m. It is first kisses and the last day of school and taking goofy pictures with all your pals.

Hell is being between a cracked puberty voice and a real voice. Hell is acne. Hell is curfew. Hell is crushes that don't like you back, the inability to handle big things like sex and your future but still having to make a lot of decisions about those things. Hell is when you and your parents stop speaking the same language. Hell is trying to fit in when everybody's too aware of things changing but too green to know how to react to them, too hormonally confused to be empathetic, and too young to be anything but selfish. And, you know, a lot of kids handle this by being assholes.

For me, high school got off to a bit of a rough start. The fall I entered high school, there was no denying I had gone from having "baby fat" to "regular girl fat." When you are in high school and you are a girl, you can be a number of horrible things: you can be a nerd, you can be a slut, you can be fat, or I guess you can be a serial murderer. I suppose if you were attractive enough, nobody would care about the last one. These things are usually dictated by some high school Smurf boy in eight popped collars who spends more time spraying AXE on himself than thinking about the feelings of other humans. But these Golden Boys have been deemed the ultimate deciders, and they decided that fat girls are gross. Gross, it seemed, I was.

If genetics do play a part in weight gain then I wasn't necessarily predisposed to obesity, but I was predisposed to a desire to not want to leave the couch, and to think Taco Bell cheese sauce tasted good. At fourteen years old, I didn't have a healthy lifestyle, and while my parents fed me vegetables and tried to get me to move around, I simply wouldn't. I had to play the *The Sims* and make large gay families. I had to watch *TGIF* while eating pints of Phish Food at my friend Amy's house. I had to trade my turkey sandwiches for the bag of piss-colored sodium that is known as Cup Noodles. At fourteen years old, I didn't have sex; I didn't kiss anybody; I didn't drink or do drugs. My vices were foods in mass quantities and sitting around.

This showed. It showed because I couldn't really fit into any of the juniors clothes besides the really unflattering Old Navy denim or khaki capri pants. All the cute juniors clothes ended at size twelve. It showed in the kind of weight gain that led a doctor to tell me I was at risk for diabetes, which scared me enough to want to change a little bit.

Of course, this wasn't the real reason I wanted to lose weight. The truth is, fifteen-year-old girls want to be skinny because it is considered socially acceptable and conventionally attractive to be thin, and people treat you better. And while I firmly believe that fat women can be beautiful, feel confident and sexy, and are human beings, this just isn't the case in high school. There's a certain currency that comes along with being thin, and you can buy a hell of a lot more with it than by being the fat girl. And at fifteen, all you are looking for is the cool kind of currency, the kind of currency that gets you invited to parties.

The summer before I became a sophomore, after a whole year of staying home alone instead of going to dances and a season ahead of rejecting pool-party invitations (not that I was getting any), I decided to go on a diet. The real tipping point for me was this neighbor who came over one day when I was practicing piano. She looked at me sitting on the bench, turned to my mother, and told her, "She would be such a beautiful girl if she lost some weight."

Ah, a big spoonful of the classic bullshit. They could be pretty IF. They could be beautiful WHEN. It wasn't that beautiful was thin; it was that beautiful could ONLY be thin. So I set out to be thin.

The first time I became thin, I did it in a very boring and very healthy way. I stopped sitting around; I joined track; I ate vegetables instead of all the things I wanted to eat.

By the start of junior year, I had lost thirty pounds. Call me Jasmine on a giant sentient carpet, because this was a whole new fucking world for me. Doors were opening everywhere . . . When I say this was exactly like the part when Cher Horowitz goes down the stairs in that *dress*, I mean it wasn't like that. It was MUCH BETTER.

Friday nights were no longer spent at home, watching the extended cut of *Pearl Harbor* or O-Town in *Making the Band*. I'd slap on an Abercrombie & Fitch T-shirt in navy blue, no doubt bearing some catchy play on words, pop on a homemade hemp choker and some Havaianas, and head out to see some friends. I say "friends" because I had actually made a group of them, the kind of in-between popular and marginally popular kids that listened to the Beatles and pretended they were from 1963. Wherever we were, we watched R-rated movies, contemplated raiding the parents' fridge for beer, and ended up by the lake at midnight, eating fast food and having crushes on each other.

I felt like this was the life I was entitled to. Being skinny meant people asked me what was "going on with Dan" instead of poking my stomach in between gym class or otherwise ignoring me. Being skinny meant cute white ruffle skirts and being desired, and all I had to do, really, was worry enough that I wouldn't change my habits. I worried that the couple of French fries I ate would go straight to my ass and stomach in the form of ten pounds. I worried that eating anything but egg whites at a diner would kill me, so I happily paid the dollar extra for them. *Even though paying a dollar extra to have them use less food is insane.* I worried that real butter or 2 percent milk was the devil, so I stuck to that gaseous butter spray and skim. This all seemed like a small price to pay for being cool and cute.

I also began to weigh myself often. I had grown up severely fearing the scale, because the scale meant the doctor's office or hating myself for gaining even more weight, but lately I had only seen decreasing numbers, and so the scale was my best friend. My mother kept this yellowing batteries-required relic of the eighties underneath her bed because she wasn't really one to weigh herself. She bought it when she was pregnant and sort of forgot about it. But I didn't. I would run up to her room, kick off my shoes, and wait the five-second lag for the electronic numbers to appear.

This either made the rest of my day great, or made the rest of my day shit. No two ways about it. Actually, it either made my day great or filled my day with me going up and down the stairs, back and forth to the scale to weigh myself again. Even one pound up would set off the pattern. First, I'd take off all my clothes. When that didn't work, I waited until I went to the bathroom. Then, I weighed myself within five minutes, ten minutes, or an hour after going to the bathroom. If that didn't work, I'd wait until the morning, when I had no food in my stomach.

Nobody told me that weighing yourself thirty times a day was an unhealthy habit, or that it was a warning sign that I was becoming obsessed with weight loss, because it's normal for a woman to weigh herself. There are commercials, whole television episodes, T-shirts, and delightfully sassy magnets in card stores devoted to a women's hatefuck with the scale. That would be my magnet, by the way—a picture of me just screaming "I hatefuck my scale" with about thirty quarts of Crystal Light pouring out of my eyes and ears. It's just accepted, kind of like the way chocolate commercials are trying to convince us that women totally love eating chocolate slowly and sensually. Like we want to bang chocolate. So I didn't think it was a problem. I didn't think I had a problem because I thought the worry about gaining weight, the constant vigilance of eating healthy, and the obsession with all of it were side effects of being thin.

Until I gained five pounds.

A couple of weeks into the summer of my junior year, doing all the BBQ things you do in the summer and having too much fun with friends to be so vigilantly tied to the scale, I paid the "ultimate price." Now, at this point in my life, I can probably gain five pounds in a weekend. It would be the easiest challenge in the world: just give me a couple of plates of nachos, three or four margaritas, Netflix, and some snacks and you've got yourself a fiver, maybe a sixer, if I'm feeling motivated enough. But that wasn't how I was then—I was a teenager. Little things threw me off the ledge. My mom looking at me a certain way could produce so much fire and rage in me that I could star in my own *Carrie* remake.

So five pounds was a very, very big deal to me. I could see myself becoming fat again, and the fatness scared me much less than being ostracized scared me.

This was something I never could get a grasp on. *Fat* was a scary word, but I don't remember when it became that way. I had never ever really been bothered by the fat I had as a kid. It was something I gripped a lot—I remember being at the dentist, getting teeth extracted, and grabbing my sides, and how comforting that was. I had a good relationship with my fat, internally. It allowed me nachos, and an extra layer of comfort. Externally, the world was against it, so I had to combat it.

What bothered me was the *badness* of being fat. The fear of it grips us. We worry about it so often, standing sideways in front of the mirror, pulling in our stomachs, talking about food like it's contraband. The badness of being fat haunted me. It said I wasn't pretty enough, or light enough, or willing to sacrifice enough to be skinny.

The only solution was to punish myself. Bulimia and I, we went hand in hand. We were a match made in the sickest kind of purgatory, a match made for the cold light of the fridge and the cold floor of a bathroom, an absolute made-for-each-other couple. People who have truly had one kind of eating disorder will tell you why they didn't have another kind of eating disorder. Anorexia, for me, was too noticeable. My parents would have noticed me not eating. I didn't have the stamina for it. I didn't have the self-restraint, I told myself, which ultimately led me to hate myself more.

Stupid fat kid wanted the cake, wanted the cake to eat it, too.

A week after I had gained those measly five pounds, I ate

a giant meal. I don't remember what it was and it hurts too much to think of what it could have been: my mother's lovingly prepared meat loaf or pasta or my favorite chicken potpie. But I do remember that what happened next was surprisingly easy. It took hardly a second. I was absolutely, positively hooked.

Here is what I have to say about bulimia:

Bulimia is a lonely disease. It is lonely to have to hide something, to eat alone and in secret, to slip off into the bathroom unnoticed while the world swirls indifferently around you. It was me, in the kitchen at two a.m., mechanically eating handfuls of anything I could get into my mouth, just so I could justify throwing it up.

Bulimia is not an *indulgent* disease. I didn't just treat myself to a triple cheeseburger at a restaurant and get rid of it. I didn't just *want* to eat; I *had to* eat. I was so surprised how quickly the problem got out of control. At first, I just wanted to lose weight but also eat whatever I wanted. I missed the foods I had deprived myself of. But quickly, oh so quickly, I became a complete glutton. I would eat when I wasn't hungry, when I wasn't craving anything. I would eat handfuls of old spaghetti, not even microwaved. Slabs of cheese, or wheat thins and cream cheese, followed by bread and butter. Handfuls of granola and handfuls of crackers and handfuls of everything. I wanted the mechanical, emotionless shovel of food in my mouth. All I cared about was the end result. I ate all the leftovers I could because nobody cared about missing leftovers, and nobody noticed me taking them. So often I wanted to be noticed. So often I wanted somebody to see me as sick, in need of help, as skinny. I just wanted it to be worth it, but I still hid, because I didn't think I was.

Bulimia never feels worth it. You do lose weight, but damn

it, you're still chubby. I was my skinniest with diet and exercise, not when I was keeping down only one meal a day. It becomes less about weight and more about the addiction itself, the fleeting satisfaction of eating a ton of stuff and never paying for it. I never even threw up all my meals; I thought this meant I was in control. Bulimia doesn't feel worth it when it becomes a compulsion that you can't keep track of. Sometimes you eat something and feel fine. Sometimes you eat for days and don't feel a thing. Sometimes you have a bite of candy and it is all downhill from there. So I was bulimic, I was still the same weight I had always been, and I was very, very out of control.

Bulimia is disgusting. It is absolutely vile to get pieces of spaghetti or old food in your hair. It is gross, very gross, to watch the different colors of your fresh meal littered into the toilet, splashing the sides of the bowl and sometimes the toilet paper dispenser and also the walls. It feels like a massive waste, because it is. You get the vomit all over your hands, and you have to clean the toilets up and down to make sure you don't leave a mark. I spent a large portion of my formative years with my face in all different kinds of toilets—public restrooms, dorm toilets, friends' toilets, my own toilet. The public restrooms were the absolute worst. I had to wipe them down first, wipe them of their shit or period blood or the misplaced piss, just so I could throw up inside them. I wasn't a rock star. I wasn't the cool kid. I was just a girl who spent most of her time cleaning toilets so she could dirty them with grilled chicken, Cheetos Puffs, and the easiest to get rid of—ice cream. It would end up on my shirt. Toilet water splashed onto my face. My eyes watered and mascara would pour down from them. Bulimia is not fucking glamorous.

Bulimia also makes you a selfish piece of shit. I will never forget the burden I put on my best friend in college by finally telling her I had bulimia. It's not a special secret to share. It's a way to get validation for your suffering, regardless of how that affects the person you tell. I was looking for somebody who wouldn't tell and who had her own problems that we could bond over. We were like two sick plankton on the whale of our shitty histories. All we wanted to do was be sick, together. I told her not to relieve my burden; I wanted to share it with somebody who would see how sick I was. When I told her, all it did was give her headaches. Rarely was I crying for help. I was crying to be sick with somebody else.

She had to watch me at all times. I remember her, lightly knocking on the door after our Friendsgiving, asking what I was doing. She slipped off, unnoticed, while everyone was digesting pie and green bean casserole and mashed potatoes. The light knock of "why" and "still?" I had promised a million times I would stop. I had promised to go to the college-provided therapy. I had promised these things to a girl who had her own things to worry about. She carried the worry of my own pain, and I let her, with the promise that she would be the one who would see me get better. I hate that I told her with no reason other than to have somebody to tell. I never had any intention of stopping, no matter how long our conversations went on, even deep into the night.

I was selfish because I didn't think of my parents or family, who had to watch me get more paranoid, and more mean, and be unsure of why. I feel selfish knowing that they will read this and know how sick I was, and I feel guilty knowing they will feel they were responsible for it.

I was selfish because I chose being sick over being anything else. Bulimia makes you angry at the world. I didn't understand what pulled me toward the toilet when I swore I would stop. I swore I would stop a handful of times during the four or so years I was actively bulimic. Sometimes I would stop for days and weeks, almost months. And then I would find myself alone with some leftover pesto pasta in the fridge and there I was, all over again. Friday at two a.m. with a stomach full of acid. Slipping into restaurant bathrooms. Holding my own hair back. Waiting for when I could flush the toilet again so the rest of the vomit would go down.

I became a wonderful, astute liar while I was bulimic. I could con my way out of everything. "I was in the bathroom for so long because I am feeling sick." I was always having a tummy ache, or a particularly brutal period, or even diarrhea. Something was always wrong with me. I lied to my parents, my friends, and anybody who would ask me "how I was." I would always respond with "good."

I was addicted to the promise of being skinnier, and it clouded every amount of good sense I've ever had. There is a certain pull to eating disorders because they are easy. It's easier not to eat than to eat healthy and work out. It's easier to throw up junk food than to give it up. It's easier to feel sick than to deal with your issues. It's easier to face nothing, to deteriorate quietly rather than get up in the morning, make the bed, and face the day.

Lastly, bulimia robs you of your beauty. I saved this one for last, because it's the only thing that truly got me to stop throwing up my food.

For years, whenever I told people why I stopped being bulimic, I said it was because I threw up blood. This is not true. I never threw up blood. I stopped being bulimic because it made me ugly. After years of turning my insides in and out, in and out, it began to show. I lost the curl in my hair. I had wanted straight hair for years, but not the scraggly, knotty, half-wave it had become. I started thinning at the crown. My mom noticed it when I was sleeping. Always the liar, I told her it was because I was dyeing my hair too much. It wasn't. My skin started to sag and dry out, too, and my nails got weakened to the point you could bend them. I was sucking the vitamins out of myself as rapidly as I was putting them in, and it showed. My skin was ashy; my stomach began to protrude from lack of nutrients. I became ugly, and for a girl who spent years trying to trick herself into looking beautiful, it was a hit to the mouth.

When I began to recover, nobody knew—because here's the thing. Nobody ever really knew I had bulimia, because you would never have known it from looking at me. I was just a girl, four feet eleven and a size 2 (a totally normal size), with straight hair always in a ponytail and some bags under her eyes. I never looked as sick as the girls I had read about, been warned about. I always looked normal. I ate with everybody at every meal.

The rot was on the inside.

I'm not ashamed that looks made me start recovery, because they made me recover.

Recovery was long, and almost restless. I had to reintroduce the concept of food into my life, because I had treated it like a medicine and a drug for much longer than it needed to be. I had to look at food as a means to survive, and then I had to learn how to enjoy it. I felt like I had lost the memory of it—what it felt like to eat a piece of cake, savor it, and let it sit in your stomach while you fell asleep. I hadn't felt full in such a long time. I was so used to feeling empty.

Recovery went so slowly. I began to eat very healthily, which helped me lose weight, even. I started running and dropped about ten pounds, and everybody told me how good

I looked. I cut all my hair off and started watching it grow back healthier, not just in length but in volume and in curl. My hair became curly again. My teeth became white again, and my skin lost its dry patches save for the harsh winter months. For a while, I didn't gain any weight. I was skinnier than I was when I was sick. I regimented my food by eating whole grains and fresh vegetables from the farmer's market. I told people I hated doughnuts, which was true because though I loved them, I hated throwing them up. I never had bagels. I was healthier than I had ever been, and happier than I had remembered, but I still was terribly afraid to gain weight.

I went to therapy, a little, but it was talking with other women that saved my life, and it still saves my life today.

I will never forget the first time I, a recovering bulimic, told a girl I had bulimia. Her face lit up like a fucking Christmas tree. "Me, too!" she said. Oh, how many "me, toos" I have heard in my life, once I started to talk. I've met girls who ended up in the hospital, who ate only a burrito a day, who lost their hair in huge clumps. We talk about how much we sometimes still want to lose weight. We talk about how good it feels to be healthy. We talk about worry; we swap stories. It is easier to find other bulimics than you think.

It started making me realize why we used to be the lost girls. Why we decided to become found.

I was bulimic because I let the importance of looking good almost kill me. I was bulimic because being sick was better than being fat. I didn't just pull that notion out of thin air: we have long since lauded the idea of diets and restrictions. The waif beauties we see, the pride in showing rib cages, the purity bestowed on the women who abstain. Abstaining has always been beautiful in a woman's world: abstaining from sex, from dessert, from food, from everything. Bulimia happens because of how bad, how awful, we treat people who are fat. Bulimia happens because losing weight results in a compliment.

I had bulimia. I am the absolute extreme. But I am not the only woman in the world to suffer from disordered eating. Disordered eating doesn't have to mean you throw up your food, or stop eating for days at a time. It could mean extreme guilt when you eat a taco or a big meal. It could mean skipping lunch often because it means you can have a big dinner. It could mean looking at food as the enemy. It could mean eating a ton because you're sad, or angry, or upset. It could mean eating so much you can't stop. It could mean feeling bad when your stomach is full. It could mean being so regimented, so healthy, you are afraid to eat something you enjoy. It is eating without enjoyment.

I have been recovered for years, *years*. I still have a horrible gag reflex, so I can never forget who I once was. I often feel like I am standing in the sun, waiting for the clouds to roll in. I am so worried about being caught in the darkness again, about losing all restraint at two a.m. It hasn't happened, but there are times I worry because even though I've changed, it's not like the entire world has come along for the ride. I still look around me and see all the different Perfect Bodies I always wanted. I only hope we can all be strong enough to fight it, or realize that fat isn't the worst thing somebody can be.

Today, I am twenty-one pounds heavier than my lowest weight, and I am up two dress sizes. I still have "fat" days. I still get nervous about looking chubby in photos. I still chastise myself for eating too much during a weekend of fun. But I like things about my body that I didn't like about it before: that it is here, and I survived. I feel lighter in ways I never did before: hopeful, happy, honest. Five years later, here's what I've learned: The perfect body is my body, because it isn't hurting anymore. The perfect body is mine because it is alive and moving. I only wish I didn't have to find this out the hard way.

Even now, the feeling of food in my stomach is a joy unparalleled. Or the joy of looking into the mirror, shirt off, and feeling like I am okay. It is the little victories of keeping any food I want in my house, of finishing when I am stuffed, of no longer wanting to drown, of being okay. And when the waiter comes, mid-meal:

"How's the food?" he asks.

"Perfect," I say. And I put my fork down, and it's okay, and I am a world away from the old familiar pangs of darkness.

Instead, I just feel full.

Advice I've Received as a Woman

I

The first advice I truly remember receiving is *don't touch things that aren't yours.*

I was a sticky-fingered little baby who had a penchant for breaking things. I broke almost everything that came into my hands. Give me something, and it would come back to you snapped in two or three. I did this to small things: pretzel rods, action figures, crayons, and pencils. I did this to bigger things: my grandfather's gift to my brother of stuffed frogs playing the maracas comes to mind. I have to point out that these were stuffed frogs as in *taxidermied* frogs, wearing sombreros and playing violins as well as the maracas. My grandfather, as demonstrated by his gift giving, was not around children for much of his life. One afternoon I went into my brother's room and climbed his bed to reach a dresser that contained the stuffed frogs, a signed baseball, and, I believe, the *Star Trek Enterprise.*

I reached for the frog and grabbed the little hand holding the bow and snapped it off. Then, I left.

My parents, tired of my destructive hands, sat me down. "Don't touch things that aren't yours." I continued to break my own things. I had almost a compulsion to destroy, something that I wish I had realized sooner than writing this, as it would have certainly ended up in my college fiction writing. No real reason for it other than I liked the snap. I broke the tails off many of my Littlest Pet Shop dogs and cats. I broke Polly Pockets and my rulers and the buttons off my shirts. I tapered off breaking things after I lost too many of my toys to my own hands. But first I learned to not touch things that weren't mine to touch. You could say this is when I learned restraint. Any time I gave in to my urge and broke something that belonged to somebody else, I lost a friend. You didn't just get to *do* the things you wanted to do, all the time. If you did, the consequence was that people didn't like you.

Instead of a grubby-handed monster, I turned into a more civilized kindergartner. I kept my hands mostly on my lap. You keep your odd compulsions to yourself so people don't get mad at you.

The second piece of advice I remember the most:

If a boy is mean to you, he probably likes you.

Boys pushed and shoved me and pulled my hair. It was meant as some sort of compliment. Greg, a second grader with a bowl cut, used to stand behind me and poke my back. Justin was the worst. Justin used to knock me off the monkey bars. With dirt-stained knees, I would defiantly tattle on him to the school monitors.

The punishment by a school monitor was a shake of the head to Justin. To me: he *likes* you. A wink.

A *wink?*

This baffled me. The things I could not touch: *definitely* stuff belonging to other people. I know this because I had wanted to rip the buttons off other people's shirts, and I knew I was not allowed to. I know this because I wanted to shove Justin back, to knock him into the ground. I still didn't do it. My mother has told me a story about how this boy put a thumbtack on her seat when she was younger, and how much it hurt when she sat on it, and how she always knew the boy had done it because he had a crush on her. But *Mom*, I want to say. I felt so bad for my mother, and ultimately even worse for myself. I wanted boys to know that doing these things shouldn't be excused. I wanted them to reel it back because they knew the consequence. I wanted them to know they couldn't use their hands like I couldn't use mine.

For three whole days, I hid in the coat closet while the other students went to lunch. I went into Justin's cubbyhole and stole every single marshmallow from his Lucky Charms, leaving only the powdery crumbs and the dry cereal. If he was gonna push, I would destroy him. He cried, and I don't know this for sure, but I remember trying to insinuate that perhaps his mother didn't love him enough to leave them there.

Justin never learned not to push. I became adept at silence and leaving my hands on my lap. Always thinking. Always wondering how to have a voice when nobody would be the voice for me.

From then on, all the way up to adulthood: I kept my hands to myself. I always wonder who has been taught to do the same, and I prepare to fight differently, quietly, swiftly, instead.

II

When I was younger, my parents got two calls about me from teachers. One was from Mrs. Bailey, a frazzled teacher who had little patience with children. This was an interesting quality from a teacher not in a Roald Dahl book, as was her general lack of interest and sternness. Mrs. Bailey had called my parents up with *concerns* about me. *Concerns* was usually code for "biting" or "let's try medication." My parents called back with the kind of trepidation that accompanies the worry that their kid will need to wear a muzzle.

The real issue? Apparently, I kept raising my hand during class. I raised it a lot. I answered only when I was called on. That wasn't the issue. It was the hand raising itself. That was the *concern*.

"She's intimidating the other students."

Perhaps I was intimidating Sam, who fell headfirst from the monkey bars almost every time we had recess. But he seemed happy enough just to sit by his desk and pick his nose. Perhaps I was intimidating Mike, a sharp-faced wunderkind who had a habit of yelling things out of turn. *He* continued to spend the rest of the year shouting the answers out. Did he get a phone call? I don't know. You sure wouldn't know it by his constant interruptions. My parents were reluctant to tell me all this, but because Mrs. Bailey did that teacher-y threatening thing teachers are so good at, they felt like they had to. I believe the phrase was "if this kind of behavior continues . . ." What? I would go to college or something?

Anyway, right after this conversation we got split up into groups for reading, and I pretended to read really slowly. I thought I would be less intimidating that way. I stuttered and stammered through words that I knew. It just felt like the right thing to do.

After I got tired of that, I just stopped raising my hand as much. It took me years to forget that lesson.

Only one year later, I had another teacher call my parents.

I had eaten "too much food at the picnic." Technically, this was true. I certainly spent most of the time housing sour cream and onion chips because, morally, I was against tug-of-war. Plus, I never got ridged chips in my sack lunch. Maybe a Cape Cod snack pack every once in a while, or an apple. But never ridged chips.

"She ate too much!" But there's *one picnic a year, lady*. Did I learn something? Oh, maybe. Next year at the picnic, I just ate in secret, so as to not offend anyone.

Be quiet. Eat less. This was the advice, really. I mean *come on.*

III

I was sitting on my grandmother's couch, or more specifically on my grandmother's lap. I was young, probably about eight. We had been living in my grandmother's house for the summer because we were building our new house a couple of towns over. I had no real friends. My grandmother made me sandwiches and I watched *Rugrats* or Nick Jr. until the sun set. She didn't mind that I hated being outside, or that I only went to Bible camp for one day. I raced home, tired, and said I didn't need to sit in a tent with a bunch of people who swatted at flies and role-played the biblical times, which was chock-full of sibling murder. She was of the belief that everything her little grandchild did was cute, and I was inclined to believe her.

In this particular moment cradled on her lap, I showed her the new move I had learned recently, perhaps from my brother, whose primary job was to show me things that would get me in trouble. This move was giving the middle finger.

"Is it bad?" I say.

She thinks.

"Yes. Well, you can get in trouble for doing it. But if you like doing it, and you don't do it to be mean, then you can go right ahead. *You can express yourself however you like. You should express yourself however you like.*"

I sat there, thinking about this. People had so often told me to be quiet, and I liked this alternative. I giggled and waved my middle finger around some more. I enjoyed the freedom of expression.

The next day, my aunts and uncles came to visit. When they left, I shouted, "Good riddance!" and gleefully ran up to my room. Later, I would give the middle finger to somebody and get in trouble for it, but in my mind, all I was doing was expressing myself. I would always mean what I said.

I liked the way I sounded when I spoke from my gut.

IV

I threw a birthday party when I was six and invited one of the girls from class whom I liked the most, probably because she was the most popular. I remember Danielle because she was very Italian in that effortless, chic way. I'm talking "straight from Long Island" cool. She wore tiny gold hoops and black floral before Forever 21 even existed in my world. I, as always, was three years behind in maturity. I still am, considering I am twenty-six at the time of this writing and still shop primarily at Forever 21.

We unwrapped all the presents after eating pizza on themed paper plates, before eating themed ice cream cake. Danielle handed me her present, which was in black-and-gold shiny wrapping. This was the sexiest wrapping paper I had ever seen. Usually all my gifts were wrapped in the kind of paper that made you *know* there were gonna be dolls in the box, but this was something different. Exciting.

And there sat in front of me: a pair of black lace panties. If I opened a pair of black lacy panties now, at my age, I would probably throw them in the bottom of my underwear drawer and only take them out when I had let my laundry pile grow so large, the air pressure would change if you climbed to the top of it. I mean, if I want to feel sexy I'll just put on a pair of Spanx, which cuts off enough circulation to my brain that I believe I am sexy.

As a six-year-old, I had a never-ending supply of *Animaniacs* Underoos and a mother who washed them for me. I didn't need an emergency pair of lacy black panties. Also, I was *six*. I could not comprehend their "message," but I was pretty confident they weren't for my age demographic. I stared at Danielle, and Danielle's mother, who was also there, and apparently fine with this present.

Better get used to them now! You'll need 'em when you get older!

This kind of reasoning haunts me. When will one *need* lacy lingerie? This was one of those first moments, those times I started to pick up on what makes a woman *sexy*. I heard snippets of things that led me to believe it was my duty as a woman to one day be a sexual being. I didn't even know what sex was, but I knew that one day, I would have to *become something*. I knew it when people asked me if I had kissed any boys yet. I knew it when people told my brother he would have to protect me because I was so pretty. And I knew it when I got a pair of lace panties for my birthday.

Later on, my mother threw them out.

"It's inappropriate!" she said.

Years later, I still don't wear lace panties, and I think it's because I didn't start early enough. Also, they really seem like they itch.

V

If I were asked to describe my grandfather, I would say two things. One was that he was over six feet tall. The second thing is that when I was nine, he told me a story about how he threw an axe at someone's head and he regretted it. Why?

"Because I missed."

I feel this description is more than enough. My grandfather came into my life in brief periods that stressed my mother out. He would never hold back, but not in the way that people say that as a compliment. Since he lived in San Juan, I only saw him once every two years. At this point in my life, I was pleasantly chubby, in the kind of way that was in fact unpleasantly chubby because everybody made fun of me. When I was fourteen, he came over to my house and we made dinner. It was something with green beans, which I hate. I remember joking that I would rather have a candy bar, which was certainly a half-joke at best.

"You should eat less. If you keep eating like that, you won't be able to fit through the door," he said.

Man, the stuff that sticks with you, sticks with you.

VI

Learn to cook because you'll make a man very happy one day!

I had been told this, in different ways, ever since I was very young. I had been told this when I helped my mother with the cupcake mix. I had been told this when my mother made a particularly delicious dinner for a large group of people. I had been told about "a Man" for much of my young life, even though I had no idea who he was. "A Man" wasn't any man, like a man you would see on the street. "A Man" was *the* man. I wasn't sure how to find him or go about looking for him. All I knew was that when I found him, I'd have to cook for him. I also had to clean up after him, because he was extraordinarily messy.

When I was eleven, every once in a while we would have family dinner at my father's cousin's house. Maggie would make pizza with her bare hands, with dough from scratch. She would take flour and water and oil and yeast, liquids and powders that looked like they would repel each other, and she would make magic from them. Maggie would spread flour on the countertop like it was fairy dust, and slowly her hands would circle the mess it made until it became a solid mass. She covered it with a gingham tea towel, and I would sit right by the tea towel and wait until it rose. I would peek, determined to see it double in size. She would swat me away. After what seemed like hours, she would add the stewed tomatoes on the top—red orbs from San Marzano, which I thought was a store, crushed with her hands and simmered with garlic, sliced so thin I could see right through them. Then came the fresh mozzarella, fresh basil torn from the garden. If I was lucky: meatballs, rolled from beef and pork, served last night for dinner, cut in half and put on top.

Plates would be passed, and she would pull things out of the fridge that she had left over because she always made too much for fear that there wouldn't be enough food. Chicken parm, *pasta alla nonna*, salads, tortellini, anything. And we would all eat, together. My brother, my mom, my dad, and the handful of I-cannot-even-figure-out-how-they-were-related-to-me who were there would sit, stuff our faces, and leave.

Maggie, at the time, was unmarried. She wasn't cooking for a man, *the man*, but for us. A lot of my family members did that. It was a currency I learned a long time ago, when my mother or grandmother would cook—to make a meal as a sign of love. When I learned to cook, I did it because I liked to feed people, but also because it felt very good. To turn on the water, to add olive oil to a pan and let it sizzle, to drain and chop and simmer and boil made me feel connected, to my roots, to my heritage, to my family and friends. To cook, even if it is for a man, is to feel that closeness. When I cook, I cook to have the leftovers in the fridge for anyone who would want them.

VII

In high school, my guidance counselor asked, "Are you sure you want to do something creative, or would you rather be a journalist?" I went to a WASP-y high school with a lot of accolades, and journalism looks good on ya, especially when the other option is starving artist.

Junior year, I had a real granola-crunch teacher, who let us call her Jill and named her kid Falcon, or something. She asked me what I was thinking of doing for college, because I was lucky enough to attend a school where that was a question you could ask without any prompt. I said, "Journalism," and then paused. "Or comedy writing."

She smiled. "We need more women saying the things on their minds! Women never get to be as funny as men." She said everything in an us-versus-them kind of fashion, like when she fought the PTA for complaining when we read *Beloved*, of all things. She let us read it anyway, because it was an important book.

Meanwhile, I went to drama class and my teacher, Mr. Fried, told me to project when I speak.

"I can't hear you! Stop *mumbling*!"

I took it all to heart.

VIII

My grandmother was a big fan of Jesus Christ. My grandmother's advice when I was younger was: Eyebrow maintenance is akin to godliness. Groom your eyebrows. Thicker eyebrows are better. Don't fight the shape of your eyebrows, but tweeze them when you can. She would sit by the kitchen table and read *Reader's Digest* and dip her saltines into coffee and tell me to always, always pay attention to my eyebrows. At that time, I only had one eyebrow, but I think she figured I would work out that situation at some point.

I had always had the kind of relationship with Jesus that was more arm's length than anything else. A superstitious child, I believed in him and any other deity, just in case one of them was King and, this way, I wouldn't be sent to hell for not getting it right.

My grandmother was the only preacher I ever had. She would sit by my bed and tell me stories of how God turned people into salt. How when you die, you had to watch a video of your life from start to finish. How much Jesus loved me. The Great Salt God loved me, even if I didn't love him, she would say.

"Okay," I would say. And she would move on.

She was an extraordinarily kind woman, a woman of God

who most notably sat bedside by a man dying of AIDS after his parents had abandoned him. She would never really give me advice about how to be a good person. That's because she thought it came naturally to people. My grandmother's advice: enjoy beer. Women should drink beer. She would make my mother bring her Budweiser, but it would be covered in a blanket, and she wouldn't drink it in front of me. She would drink it, probably, by the portrait of Jesus on the side wall. Jesus was her pal. He died for her because they were buddies, and she liked the types of lessons he taught. But she let me know that it wasn't shameful to enjoy a beer, to enjoy life.

I don't quite know how I feel about Jesus, but I love my grandmother. After she passed: my eyebrows are always perfect. I try to be nice, too.

IX

Advice I received when I was in college, with varying degrees of importance and accuracy:

Be careful how much bleach you put in your hair. You can cut your own bangs. Sleep in as late as you can. You should rim your eyes in black eyeliner. If you have to pull an all-nighter, do a face mask to keep from breaking out and do not, under any circumstances, take a nap. Sure, you can wear that sweatshirt three days in a row to class. One cigarette won't kill you. Take notes. Another cigarette won't kill you. Don't make it a habit. Condiments don't expire. If waffles are an option, get the waffles. Don't buy textbooks. You can finish a paper in an hour if you try hard enough. Keep your vodka in water bottles. Keep a condom in your purse. Don't keep a condom in your purse because the oils from the purse will ruin the condom and the condom won't work. Put milk instead of water in the Easy Mac. Sleep around, but don't be offended when the guy doesn't call you back. Don't sleep around, it's gross. Oh, don't go home with him, it's gross. Don't be like Lisa, she's gross. Books over boys. Befriend other women. Don't brag. Be quiet. Be loud. Pluck. Try the Diva Cup. Try experimenting sexually for a while, something might stick. Do your homework. Don't drink Mad Dog 20/20. Learn something. Enjoy it while it lasts.

The most useful: you should try reading more books by women, and if you rub your tights on deodorant marks, they come right off.

X

The advice I've received most in life, hands down, is to moisturize my neck.

I have been told this advice with great urgency throughout my whole life. Each year, I hear it at least twice more than the last. I have received this advice by the same people on multiple occasions, and it's still delivered like they had never told me this advice before.

"You have to moisturize your neck." My mother is watching me put lotion on my face before I get ready for bed.

"I know, Mom." I inch upward toward my forehead instead.

"Because if you don't, your neck gets wrinkly." She's coming closer to me now. I push the bottle just out of her reach, lest she get any wild ideas.

"I know. I moisturize my neck." After slathering my face, I rub my neck with now dry hands, almost theatrically. I stare at her.

"Because, I'm telling you, your neck gets wrinkly. And then, you will regret it." She shows me her neck, which to her credit looks wonderful. She is 100 percent Puerto Rican and doesn't have my Irish genes, though, which turn skin into the kind of sponges that can scour pans.

"Your neck looks great."

"Thank you. It's because I moisturize." She starts to leave the room.

"And you're too harsh on the skin under your eyes. You have to pat your lotion instead of rubbing it in like you're trying to hurt yourself."

To her credit, this is true. I tend to moisturize like I have some sort of debt to pay. I feel like it sinks in more this way, like bad news or when you find somebody attractive and learn that he's eight years younger. My technique will scare all the wrinkles away. I will physically smooth them out.

The eye thing is the bigger problem, I feel. People tell me that eye skin is basically equivalent to tissue paper. Or equivalent to the sun, as you can't look at it directly and you can't touch it. I read this a lot in magazines. They also say you have to tap different creams underneath your eye area. I've always been a rubber and a smearer, and according to most everyone this means my eyes will look like small shar-peis by the time I am thirty-five.

The advice about tapping cream under your eyes is centered around the marketed idea that wrinkles on women are akin to small disfigurements. Have enough wrinkles, and people will start treating you like you are always late to ring your precious bell tower. Men never hear anything about wrinkles. I know this because men have them, deeply, and men are all called "distinguished" and "silver foxes" and even "weathered." Weathered, in a man's world, is a *good thing*. It means you're fit to sling wood and wear heavy flannel jackets and stand New England weather. Meanwhile, I'm over here trying desperately to prevent wrinkles, ever since I was a teenager. Anything to hold off my eventual decay into Grandmother Willowdom.

We do try to compliment those who already *have* wrinkles as graceful. I see these backhanded compliments all the time. They say you are "aging with grace," which to me sounds similar to "she checked *herself* into that institution." I know what they are getting at: you done fucked up, but we still want you to remain optimistic about your appearance so you'll still buy other creams. Wrinkles are certainly not the end of the world, and I believe can even enhance an otherwise boring face. If you hate them, you can just pump yourself full of whatever Botox is made of (silicone? Young, fresh women?). Still, prevention is big in the world of the female, and you learn early on to comply with it. You moisturize, you wear SPF, you pat your eyes, and you do it double if you're a smoker or a drinker.

I forget to moisturize my neck almost all the time. I do not know if I will regret it, yet.

XI

Don't eat all that pizza, you will get too full.
    I did. I loved eating it anyway.

XII

The most common job advice I've received: wear a pencil skirt and smile, smile, smile. Oh, and don't wear red lipstick for an interview; it's crude.

My favorite advice? Get paid, and run everyone over who stands in your way.

XIII

Don't get tattoos that will be visible in a wedding dress.

You shouldn't get a zombie pinup girl tattoo of yourself, Alida.

You shouldn't get a tattoo of a person's name unless that person is dead.

Alida, stop telling me tattoo ideas when you are drunk.

XIV

The second most common piece of advice I have received as an adult woman is along the lines of "don't get murdered." Interestingly enough, this usually comes as dating advice. "Date around a lot, honey, but be careful you don't get killed doing it." This is not so much even advice as much as it is an order, but it's usually surrounded by some tidbits that prevent the murder from taking place. I get it almost as much as the neck thing, by many people at many different times.

Women who are into men get a lot of unsolicited dating advice. Women who are into women get a lot of rude questions. They also get unsolicited dating advice for a gender they aren't even into. Most women get more dating advice than job advice. I have even been told that I should treat finding a date like finding a job, and that I need to be diligent about the whole thing.

I have also been told, lightly maybe, but I have still been

told, that there are people out there I could date who are waiting to turn me into a lamp shade. My skin, specifically. "Be careful, Alida. You never really know who's out there." To avoid becoming a lamp shade, the advice I receive is not to go home with any attractive men. Attractive men, normal men, even wonderful-seeming men turn women into lamp shades. I know this because when I was dating in New York City, my mother would tell me about all different kinds of nice-guy serial killers.

"It's always the nice ones."

When I asked more about that, she said, "It's the nice ones that you don't expect." When I asked even more about that, she said, "You can tell because they come from nice families, and they're very charismatic."

This made me afraid of most men and certainly of all the Kennedys.

"Should I date *mean* men?"

The response to this was mostly, no, I just should date men who people knew didn't have a meat freezer. Or date men who didn't wear clothing that a man in a Lifetime movie would wear. Or always "meet them in a public place." Or "find somebody who knows them. Ask for references." Of course, now that Tinder and OkCupid exist, this advice becomes a lot more complicated. References are nearly impossible, unless we start treating Tinder like an Airbnb app: *Jeff comes highly recommended. Minimal knives. I would say he had an appropriate amount of knives, none of which he ever waved at me. If only he had appreciated the Food Network and was more cautious of the location of the barbecue sauce on his face, we could have really been something.*

The advice in these dating situations is mostly just "go

with your gut." My gut isn't much of a sage. I wouldn't trust my gut to host a radio show or anything. It mostly just leads me to drinks and, usually, the kind of men who will buy them for me. People just use the gut as some sort of blanket statement when they could be wrong about something. "Do you think this dress will fit me?" *Go with your gut.* "Is this the kind of man who will *eat me*?" *Go with your gut.* "Is he wearing *tweed*?"

Men never receive advice like this. When they leave the house to meet a woman on a date, nobody says, "Dave, be careful that she doesn't want to store your head in a refrigerator." Everybody just lets Dave leave the house with very little worry about Dave at all.

I'm being unfair. If there are men reading this—my deepest apologies. Men are worried about things: that they will somehow lose their wallets, that somebody will break a bottle over their heads at a bar, that they will wake up in a bathtub in ice with their livers missing, and that a woman in their lives will definitely become Glenn Close from *Fatal Attraction*.

The last one is a very big fear.

So *Fatal Attraction* was made in 1987. It was about a woman who was mentally unstable. Since she was *already* mentally unstable, unsurprisingly she continued to act that way toward Michael Douglas after they had an affair. She wore shoulder pads, had amazing hair, and knew a fantastic recipe for rabbit stew. At the end, the wife of Michael Douglas shoots her dead.

This movie has been at the top of the "Women Are Crazy" Curriculum ever since. It proved women were absolutely bonkers. Even though Michael Douglas had a hottie wife and cheated on her with the kind of woman who murders children's animals. *Even though this movie didn't happen in real life, can you guess what the main lesson to be taken away from this film was?* Chicks are crazy. *All* chicks are crazy, and they get even more crazy at the sight of your dick. *Dick is what makes people crazy.*

Men still refer to this movie, citing the fact that, sometimes, women go theatrically crazy after you have sex with them, and will try to kill you and your children. Why is *Fatal Attraction* still the movie we refer to when we describe women as crazy? Well, since then, there have been around two movies made in this vein: *Swimfan* with Erika Christensen and *Obsessed* with Ali Larter, Idris Elba, and Beyoncé. Let's be super generous and add *Misery* in there.

Why? Because women don't go on murderous rampages *nearly enough* to make this a movie and television phenomenon. It's just not common enough to be included in the neon veins of pop culture.

Now what about men beating, murdering, hunting, or killing women? That's mostly every crime movie, horror movie, or Southern drama spanning generations ever made. It's what begins *Thelma and Louise*. It's what launched the plot of countless Lifetime movies. Every woman can point out a specific crime show in which the serial murderer goes after somebody who fits her profile. Even *romantic movies*, like that dog pile of a Nicholas Sparks movie *Safe Haven*, are based on the fact that the woman is hiding from an abusive husband. That's a cute little plot device to get Julianne Hough in the arms of Josh Duhamel!

Here's my advice when it comes to dating between men and women. Men: sometimes you get a particularly enthusiastic girl who will call you eight times when you're no longer interested. Women: sometimes you get turned into Pottery Barn merchandise.

You take your risks!

XV

They will never buy the cow if they can get the milk for free.

Never once do they consider that I might not want to be bought, and that I am not a cow at all.

XVI

So often I had heard the phrase, "you'll know when you have kids," that oftentimes I worry if I birth a child, I will be flooded with such a sense of knowledge that I will knock myself out.

XVII

Speak up, girl. What you have to say is important.

My advice:

Work your ass off. Find a shade of lipstick that you really love and pray it doesn't get discontinued. Ask someone out. If you don't want to go out on Saturday, don't, and don't feel guilty. Eat your vegetables. Say yes if the worst thing that can happen is you will fail. Learn to throw things out. Get renter's insurance. Read as many books as you can. Get a little more sleep. Take a jacket. Only say "I'm sorry" when you really mean it. Get what you really want by being authoritative and firm. Put a pinch of nutmeg in your roux. Bring extra socks when packing. Save your money. Get taxis when it is late. Go for seconds. Kiss often. Be more fearless, not more reckless. Take the steps to change. Admit when you are wrong. Buy a screwdriver. Make your bed. Pay your bills on time. Remember you are worthwhile and important. Make yourself happy.

Feral

Girls often go places in groups.

Surely, you know this. It's in Girl Humor 101. Very light, very sitcom-y fare. If you are a girl and get up and go to the bathroom with another girl in tow, a man will usually say "of course" or "haha, girls always go to the bathroom together." That's it. That is the joke. Technically, the man is right. I like to go places with my friends. I will even get manicures with my friends, even though we rarely get seated together, we never finish at the same time, and I am usually stuck there waiting while my friend sits under the light that dries her nails. There are many reasons we go places together. They aren't real big secrets. Mostly, it's common sense:

1. We need help choosing something, like an outfit or a perfume or a particular hairstyle, and need to survey the crowd for an honest opinion and then ask them to repeat this honest opinion one hundred times.

2. We are in want of mac and cheese and bottles of

wine, which usually is split between one other
woman or around fifty other women.

3. Gossip and Advice. Repeat after me: Hard Gossip
    and Unsolicited, Drunken, Raucous Advice.
4. I don't know, we want to spend some time to-
    gether? Get over it.

This is an "included, but not limited to" list, of course. Feel
free to add some more items at your own leisure.

We are often stereotyped as moving together in flocks, like
giant flamingos in peplum skirts that squawk and smell like
flowery perfumes or whatever. I remember this being the
premise of a Dane Cook joke I heard, that girls just get together
in giant circles and dance around. I often don't like to listen to
white men who yell, but he has a point I suppose. I don't necessarily take offense because whatever, I do go shopping with
my girlfriends and then go to a club where we push everybody
off the dance floor because TLC's "No Scrubs" comes on and
we need *the whole floor*. It certainly isn't what qualifies me or
you to be called a woman. Although there is some truth behind
the stereotype that women like to travel in packs.

Here are some other reasons:

1. It feels safer that way.
2. It feels safer on account of how many women get
    attacked and harassed all the freaking time.

I know, I know. I said something that makes people feel
extremely uncomfortable. Bringing up that women get attacked, and that yes, they are scared of this happening, often
incites more annoyance or anger than sympathy. It is very
weird. I apologize if you are a male and you are reading and

you happen to be very sensitive about this. I don't know why so many men get squicky when women talk about things like feeling unsafe or objectified, but hey. I'm so sorry that I said a thing that makes a dude frustrated and annoyed because he *specifically* is not attacking somebody.

I always feel like I sound so accusatory when I mention how unsafe I can feel as a woman. Mention you're scared to walk home by yourself or whatever it is, and boom. You're exaggerating. You're lying. It's really not that bad. You're making men out to be monsters. But here's what it really comes down to: it happens. Men attack women. If they didn't, *Law & Order: SVU* wouldn't have been on for a billion years with fresh material every week. And that fear is real, every single time I go out and know I will be returning home late. I hate feeling nervous. I hate feeling like I have to leave parties earlier than I want to. I hate looking behind me constantly and only breathing again when I close the door behind me. I don't think it is *all men* who attack women. It's that I just can't tell which ones are the ones who will.

When I am walking down the street at eleven p.m., checking behind me to see if the man who told me I was looking sexy is following me, the idea that I don't hate men, or that not all men attack, isn't on my mind. I have men in my life whom I love and respect, I have men whom I am indifferent to in my life, and I have men in my life whom I really dislike but am not scared of. These are not the men on my mind when I walk home at night.

I am scared that today is the day I will meet the one that doesn't fit into the "not ALL men" category. I am scared that today is the day my whole story changes. I am scared that today I will meet the man who decides to hurt me. I think about that in a very real way. A man approached me just the other day and asked me how I was doing as I was closing the door to my apartment. I said fine and when I started to turn a corner, I realized he had followed me and was walking fast toward me on a side street with nobody on it. I ran across the street and felt like I had dodged a bullet, and then I went and got a cup of coffee. That is a completely normal feeling for me. I feel like I am dodging bullets all the time. I feel like I can only dodge so many bullets before I get hit. And the truth of the matter is: I've never met a woman who wasn't scared to walk around at night.

The first woman I met who was sexually assaulted was not the last woman I met who was sexually assaulted. I've met many since. I will never be sure if someone else I love or I myself will one day be added to that list. I do worry often about the length of that list.

I wonder how many men who complain about women's fear of men have heard a story, firsthand, from one of these girls. Not on the evening news, not on the Internet where the only thing you read about her is her *after*, but in person. The story of this night people are so conditioned to reason with, to tear down. *She was drunk. It's stupid to be drunk. She was by herself. Everybody knows you don't walk home by yourself.* If men heard the story in person, would they be so willing to judge, then?

The first time a woman told me she was sexually assaulted, her eyes got glassy, but she didn't cry. She stood straight up and looked ahead. Her posture was impeccable, and her arms were crossed firmly at her chest. I have seen women casually mention sexual assault among women they feel safe with—"No thanks, I'm not drinking; I feel weird drinking after somebody dropped something in my drink a while back." I've seen women be frank about it, like it was just a fact. I've had women tell me it was their fault. I've known women who didn't want to ruin the lives of the men who assaulted them. And most of all, I have heard women be strong, facing something that is, so often, a story that a lot of women have.

Still, when I mention my fears, I'm told that I am marginalizing and generalizing and all the other words people throw my way. When I mention I don't like catcalls when I go places, they say that I'm the kind of person who is making men afraid of being nice. They say I push too far and, soon, men will have to sign a contract before they have sex with somebody so they won't get accused of rape. First of all, fucking fine with me. Make them sign it with a notary in court. Second, that will never happen in the history of the world. Third, false rape allegations are very unlikely, but if a woman is falsely accusing you of rape, wouldn't the contract be good to have in the first place? Finally, do you know how many untested rape kits sit in police stations across the country? Do you know how many rape cases are thrown out due to lack of evidence? Do you know how many women know that if they are raped, most likely nobody will believe them? The hard truth is that you *could* be a rapist in this country right now and be much more likely to get away with it than to have to sign a stupid fucking contract when you go home with a girl.

Mind you, the men who fight me on these points are sometimes the same men I trust. They throw light jokes at me, stuff like "well, don't get offended" when they make a joke about putting chloroform on a rag and making me fall asleep. But they are the same men who tell me to be safe when I walk home, too. They know I'm not always safe. Choosing to present yourself as a female in any way, whether that means tiny club dresses or sweatshirts or T-shirts, feels kind of nervewracking at many moments of the day. Every day.

This is where the idea of a pack comes in handy. When women go out on these "girls' nights" to spend time together in the bathroom or at house parties or restaurants, we often have a pretty detailed plan on how to stay together.

Creating a plan is *key*. You should never let a friend go home with someone unless you have some kind of information about the person she's with. Could be a last name, an address, a connection to a friend, secret DNA grabbed carefully from his head as he is leaving the bar, whatever. You can't let her leave with somebody if she's super intoxicated. If a friend is going off to another location with a person, she has to text us that she's okay. If it's past one a.m., she has to take a cab to go home. You have to make sure all your friends get into cabs. And most important, don't walk home alone.

Good girlfriends don't say good-bye to each other. They say "get home safe." Sometimes it's followed up with a *please text me when you get home*, or an *are you sure you can get back okay?* I have heard "get home safe" so many times in my lifetime. It's delivered almost stealthily—in my ear when I'm getting a farewell hug, a quiet murmur when I'm putting on my coat. When I leave the bar by myself, it feels like a risk, oftentimes. One in four women is assaulted in her lifetime, by the way. Why don't you take a moment to think about how many women *you* know?

The education of my safety as a woman began young. My mother used to tell me stories. When she was a kid, her mother had to chase a man out of a hallway with a broom. Be careful, she would tell me. Little girls get scooped up into cars. When I was older, she told the story about a girl who got hurt by not checking underneath her car. She described movies: *Mr. Goodbar* was a movie in which Diane Keaton meets the perfect man of her dreams who eventually kills her. She mentioned how in

The Silence of the Lambs, the girl got kidnapped for helping a handicapped person move a couch. Don't help. Keep walking. Don't let people in because they want to help you get the grocery bags up to your apartment. I learned these stories well before I ever had to use them, but when I was twenty-two and somebody asked if he could help with the groceries, I almost ran farther than Forrest.

When I was eight, we moved to a suburb that should have been called "Nothing Ever Happens Here." Still, we had a safe word for when I would walk home by myself from the bus stop to my house. It was "muffin," and anybody who asked me into a vehicle had to say it. Muffin is funny and I realize that. Nobody ever stopped me and asked me to jump into their van, but I knew that they could. My brother used to walk home by himself, too, and one time he walked on a guardrail and fell, and a bone jutted out of his ankle because of it. I worried that my parents had given all the safety advice to me and not my brother. Was it more dangerous to be a girl?

Boys will be boys, they said. But shouldn't we teach boys how to be safe, too? Shouldn't we teach them to be careful and wary of strangers and respectful of boundaries?

When I was eleven, my brother and I were hanging out in the magazine section of Barnes & Noble. A man followed us from aisle to aisle. My brother, wide-eyed, told me we had to go. I looked over at the man: corduroy suit jacket and glasses and messy gray hair. In his hand was an open magazine. There were naked women on the pages. He was following us around with porn.

The fear began to manifest more when I got older. Blame puberty, although it's not like younger children are automatically safer. The moment I grew breasts and started to become shapely, the idea of womanhood came with conditions. The second I looked enough like the way we think women look, I became a potential victim. The stories I heard began to change: the idea of leaving your drink alone entered the conversation. Learning to never walk alone. To take your friend with you. To prevent the crime before it happens. Not to get into a situation you shouldn't be in. The responsibility soon became ours.

When I went to college, I felt like the only way I could be safe was if I saw the bad guy coming from a mile away. I became vigilant. I figured everyone who was walking around was out to get me. Nobody talked to men about "here's how you can tell if a woman is consenting to have sex with you" or "here's what you shouldn't say to women when they are walking around by themselves and are afraid of you." All I knew was "prevent it," and "if you don't prevent it, you're gonna end up on the *Nightly News*, and not for something fun, like your Rollerblading pug." And that's when I learned to be truly scared. The world became more frightening the moment I went out on my own.

The easiest thing to be wary of is catcalling. Catcalling isn't always an assault, as many times it can simply be annoying. I understand the premise of catcalling: it's a way to tell a woman she's aesthetically pleasing, right? Or is it asserting your own male dominance, since you can't outright whip your dick out and spin it around in public? I implore the men of the world to say "good morning" or "hello" to a woman if they absolutely would *die* without saying something. Not, like "where's your man, baby?" as if that ever has had a rate of success. Just hello. If you are an old man or woman and you want to say good morning to me while sitting on the bench you inhabit every morning, fine. If you are someone I'm friendly with in the neighborhood, great. If you are anyone else, I'm going to take a leap here and say, "Why don't you try shutting your fucking mouth."

And for those of you who think you are being nice? Okay. Go ahead and say "lookin' good" like you're a construction worker in the world of Frank Sinatra. Say it to everyone who walks by. Say it to men. I once heard somebody (lie, I meant a lot of people) say that catcalling is a compliment on the way you look, and that we should be grateful for it. First of all: I'm not grateful. It makes me uncomfortable and it worries me. I do not give a flying fajita what you think I look like. Furthermore, most of the time I already know I look great. Women have self-confidence on occasion, and they don't need a guy on a break screaming at them while shoving a Dunkin' Donuts' egg sandwich down his fat throat to help them out with it. I *know* I look fantastic. And you certainly don't need to tell me TO SMILE. I refuse to walk down the street, listening to music, smiling like a maniac all by myself. If all the women other men have told to smile actually smiled, the world would look deranged. If you don't believe me, try this experiment: walk around your house and smile to yourself and try not to feel like there's a dead person in your freezer after twenty minutes of constant grinning.

And why do we act like everybody's all compliments and good-old-boy chivalry and harmless comments? It's not all "hey baby," it's "you're a fuckin' bitch" when you don't respond or "you want this dick???" On many occasions, it escalates fast. I've been yelled at out of cars that I'm a piece of shit for . . . what? Not wanting your mealy dick? Does anybody EVER say, "Thanks for calling me hot, I will go home with you now"? Anyway, I don't want you. I want to go to the subway or the doctor's office without getting harassed by a guy old enough to be my dad.

Rude words aren't the only problem. I don't know your intentions with these words and creepy stares. In college, on the crowded subway line going from downtown Boston to All-ston, a man who stared at me on the train platform managed to grind himself up against me while I waited to get off the train to go to a party. Then, I got off the train and gagged until I threw up. I said nothing, and neither did anybody else (we can never truly count on anybody noticing). Now, I would have screamed. I would have kicked. I think. But who really knows. On more than one occasion, I was cornered by men who pretended they were asking for a cigarette, screaming at me when I denied them anything but silence.

When I moved to New York, I was fully prepared to be "more careful." When my brother visited my apartment, he gave me the longest hug he's ever given me. *Be careful*, he said. Immediately, I felt like I had jumped into some sort of criminal Frogger game. The first apartment I lived in didn't have the best reputation: the girl upstairs got robbed at gunpoint and there was an attempted assault on my block. But that didn't make me any more nervous; it just solidified what I already knew. Strangers were out to get me. I had to keep watch, al-ways.

The trouble isn't that it's just strangers, either, or men leer-ing in dark stairways like the Halloween song in *The Nightmare Before Christmas*. We have always been warned about the men we know, too. I don't know why I was taught that even the men around us cannot possibly control themselves around women sometimes, but it is a lesson we must stop teaching. Men are perfectly able to control their bodies around us. It's insulting to men to say that they are so taken by us that they are willing to commit a crime or demean another human be-ing. When we say "not all men," men shouldn't be mad at us; they should be mad at the idea that enough men do it to war-rant the stereotype.

The advice I got the most before I left for college was "watch your drink." College boys were similar to high school boys in that they were hormonal, but with the lack of parental supervision. Without that, we had a Boys Gone Wild situation on our hands. They catcalled. They decided which girl looked hottest in short skirts. They tried to have sex with as many women as there are Solo Cups in the entire world. In college, where drinks were plentiful and consent was marred by Jell-O shots and cheap vodka in plastic handles, we took our drinks to the bathroom for fear that somebody might drop something in them and have sex with us. Instead of telling men not to rape, not to take advantage of young girls away from home, we tell women to take their drinks with them when they pee. You know, just in case. And if you screw up because you're eighteen and you're drinking Mike's Hard Lemonade? You know the consequence of leaving your drink out where someone can tamper with it: every girl knows you make one wrong move and all of a sudden you were the one who wanted it; you were the one who was promiscuous; you were the one who should have taken your drink to the damn bathroom.

I have walked through life mostly unscathed. I've had some real moments of fear, late at night. I only have one story I tell at bars, when we tell our stories at bars. My story isn't that bad, compared to others. But damn, it still hurts to tell it.

The year I graduated college, I lived in an apartment that was ten minutes from the subway station in Boston. The walk was a quiet one. In ten minutes, you passed very little. A rotary, a Dunkin' Donuts, and houses. That's it. There were few cars, fewer streetlights, and I was very aware that I could scream with no response at all. A walk like that is not ideal. I crave people. I crave bodegas that I can run into and say, "I think somebody is following me." I look for occupied streets, people walking their dogs, bars that are always open. But the walk from the Davis T stop to my house had none of that. And as a girl who worked at a coffee shop before the sun rose, there were many times I made that walk feeling like I was the only girl in the world. Hoping I wouldn't bump into the Big Bad Wolf.

Most of the time, nothing happened. Homeless men would begin to hunt through trash on Monday trash collection day, but they always nodded at me, saying nothing. I would jog to the subway on most early winter mornings when it was still dark. One time, after walking home from a friend's house, a man stood by the rotary, screaming. I called my roommate and ran past him like a track star with Red Bull wings while she came flying up on her bicycle, in her pajama shorts. I knew there were people lurking, whether they were good or bad, whether they were hiding or in plain view.

Nothing ever happened until Saint Patrick's Day. Now, you should understand that I, like most reasonable humans, already hate Saint Patrick's Day. I don't need an excuse to drink whiskey, and I don't need to kiss anybody because they are Irish, and I certainly don't need to watch three billion amateurs throwing up into city trash cans because they had beer for dinner.

So. I volunteered to work. I spent the day slinging coffee to very restrained and very sober businessmen. By all accounts, it was a good day. Afterward, I went over to my friend Colin's house for a couple of beers, a couple of shots of whiskey, and no mention of Blarney Stones or four-leaf clovers.

In case you were wondering, I was wearing all black, and it was dark. I was walking home. I don't remember the time, but it wasn't past midnight.

The first week of school, my dad had told me and my roommate about a safety class one of the school's officers was giving. Basically, it was a rape-prevention class. Let's just get that out of the way. He gave the (all-women) class some advice: one was to pretend you were talking to your boyfriend on the phone when you were feeling uncomfortable at night. This was a very "whatever" tip for me because I had been doing that forever. Having a boyfriend was always the best defense to men. Guy hitting on you that you don't want to talk to? Tell him you have a boyfriend. Don't want to get followed home? Talk to your fake boyfriend. Don't want to keep getting aggressively hit on? Say your boyfriend the MMA fighter/police officer/Dothraki is coming to meet you soon.

But another tip the officer gave, I liked. He said, "Whenever you see anyone that makes you uncomfortable, turn your headphone off but keep them in your ears so as to not draw attention to yourself." This one, I thought, was good. I found it extremely handy when I was eavesdropping on a conversation between fighting spouses, and I found it handy when I was walking home that Saint Patrick's Day.

A group of frat boys was walking toward me. Frat boys generally didn't scare me in college because many of them wore salmon-colored shorts. But they were drunk, stumbling over each other and high-fiving and missing each other's hands. There were about seven of them—between five and seven guys, maybe. They took up the whole sidewalk and could barely walk it. I remember thinking that while I saw no cars, I was still annoyed that most likely I would have to step into the street to avoid them. I turned off my headphones to anticipate the awkward "sorry, excuse me" conversation I was about to have.

About fifty feet away, I heard them talking.

I remember this: "She's wearing black. She wants it, man." One of them, I kid you not, said she's "asking for it."

What do I do? Do I run into traffic? Do I scream? What do you do? What do you do when all the precautions you take go wrong? What do you do when all your lessons must come into practice?

By the time I was done contemplating this, they had already surrounded me. A full circle. One of them grabbed my wrist. I felt another breathing behind my neck.

As somebody who is four feet eleven, I am good at getting through crowds. And the thing I learned, when I was very young, is that you can dart under a man's raised arm if you are short and quick enough.

I have used this trick when I darted underneath people to get to the front row of a standing-room-only concert. I have used this trick when a crowd was gathered outside a store upon the release of *Titanic* on two VHS tapes and I wanted to be one of the first to grab it. I have used this trick when a guy at a party pulled out a knife in the doorway amid an argument with his friend. And now, I was about to use this trick for survival, or whatever would come after they had surrounded me.

I felt one grab the back of my shirt, but I was too fast. It was my own example of fight or flight. I darted across the street and began to sprint.

Here are a couple of things before I continue: I do not deserve praise for escaping. I do not deserve props and I am not better at survival than anybody else who does not get away. There is no wrong answer for what a woman should do. No matter what her fate is, no matter what happens, she always does what she can. No matter how many times police officers, my mother, my brother, had told me to scream and punch or do what the attackers say or throw my purse into the bushes, I used pure intuition. All I remembered was how beautiful the trees looked on the other side of the street as I was running to them.

There was a man on the other side of the street, a ways up. He looked like he was waiting for me. "I saw them," he said. "They were watching you. I stopped here to see if you got away. You're very fast. Do you want me to walk you home?"

"No," I said. "Just to the end of the street, please." We walked slowly. This was 2010, when Haiti had just been struck by a devastating earthquake. The man's family still lived in Haiti, and he said while some had lost their homes, they were all alive. He worked as a cook and sent them home money sometimes. His uniform told me he was telling the truth.

"It's scary," he said. "No matter where you are, you just never know what will happen."

And that is true. Some of you will read this story and think that the boys were being boys. You will think that nothing would have come of it, just me and five to seven boys on an empty, dark street. They were drunk. They just wanted to . . . scare me? Say hi? They probably went to Tufts University, the affluent college that costs more than most people earn in a year.

And maybe they wouldn't have done anything. But I can't tell you that, because I was scared and because some men *do*. Especially when they are in college.

I think about those men often. The boys who circled me are probably around my age. They have graduated from college by now. Maybe they have good jobs and sweet girlfriends. Maybe they get irritated by feminism on Twitter. I don't know.

But I don't think of them as often as I think of the Haitian man, who had much less and offered me much more.

And I think of those boys less often than I think of all the college boys who don't know the difference between stop and go because nobody taught them about it. I want them to learn, and I want them to be taught, for the sake of their moral characters and the spirits of the girls who deserve to be kept safe.

And I think of the women these men affect, who have had their lives changed because of men who think they are entitled to just barge in and change them without asking. I think of girls who grip their cups and check behind them, and I think of one in four women, all the time. I think of all their voices, the voices that have been silenced, and the voices that have learned to speak again.

But I still think of those boys and wonder whom they will take the form of, next, and if I will ever meet men like them again.

There are good men. There are bad men. I can't tell who is who when the moon is out.

We must teach, we must learn, we must believe the people who say they are scared and who say they are hurt, and until then—

Please. Get home safe.

All the Diets I've Been On

Can you tell me a little bit about your relationship with salmon? I bet you have one. Even if you are a vegan or are landlocked, you know something about salmon, because if you are a woman, you know something about diets.

I know a lot about diets. I've eaten so much steamed fish I'm surprised I can't breathe underwater, in some sort of "you've now become one with the fish" kinda way. I've steamed broccoli within an inch of its life, even three inches past its life, until it becomes a mushy sort of stew. I've had "sandwiches" made of one-hundred-calorie bread. I would rather eat a paper plate than this bread, but that's just coming from a woman who likes things like spice and flavor in her food, and plates have more of that in comparison.

One day, I will travel upstream to the land of the salmon and stand on the rocks, thanking the fish for all they've done for us. I will lay down the many celebrity diet issues of *People* magazine, with the after-baby-weight-lost-in-only-three-months photo shoots. "Look," I will say. "Look how quickly Gisele Bündchen jumped back into shape from the baby because of your sweet flesh. Look how Jennifer Lopez stays so sexy after forty. All because of you." Then I will take a fish out of the ocean, and I will steam it without any oil and just a squeeze of lemon, and I will ceremoniously eat it in skinny jeans.

The rest will probably swim away, willingly, into the mouth of a bear, which I believe is also a lean meat. By the way, a Google search of "Gwyneth and salmon" produced 521,000 results in .30 seconds. Of course. They are a logical pairing, like "strict diets" and "no more fun." Paltrow has many different ways to make salmon. She also makes her own Sriracha. She is just like us, except less slovenly and with many more millions of dollars.

On another note, what are your feelings about egg whites? Do you ever order an all-egg-white omelet at a brunch place because you truly want to put it in your mouth? I myself have sat in many greasy spoon diners, valiantly shoveling piles of canola-oil-soaked egg whites, or "rubber-no-flavor-pain," as I have named it in my head. I have not enjoyed this. I have stared across the table at my comrades, sporting plates with the most American of cheeses lying comfortably across white bread soaked in butter, idly oozing next to crisp French fries, and I have thought of murder. *This is for my body*, I think, *not for my happiness*. Or: *You can't stab your friends with a fork and steal all their French fries, but you can at least try to steal some when they go to the bathroom.*

Can you tell me about your last diet, at least? Go with the salmon, they say. It has omega-3s and the healthy good fats and it makes your skin pretty. Wrap it in tinfoil and mince some garlic on it. Hell, put ginger on it. Serve it with green beans (no butter) or brown rice (*no butter*). You won't regret it. Your body will thank you. Trust me, I know a lot about being healthy.

I've been on diets since I was a little girl. Call it tragic. Call it a woman thing. Call it whatever you want, especially the norm.

I know all the ways you can eat as a woman: eat only chicken the size of your fist or a deck of playing cards (the size of fists varies), eat only the one lone square of dark chocolate, drink glasses of water between courses. We are always saying things before we dive into a meal—"Oh, I'm being good, I wish I could have the pasta, I'm only going to eat a little bit of this." "It's my cheat day," if it's fries. "I'm being naughty," if it's fries. When you ask for no butter, it's to keep your girlish figure. When you push the bread away from your plate and say, "I just can't," it's not because you physically can't, it's because you're not *supposed to*.

Can you tell me, then, the last time you were allowed to be totally satisfied with the way you ate? I think I had to have been about ten. When I was born, Rafiki from *The Lion King* probably rubbed that red stuff on my forehead and said, "You will learn to eat a handful of nuts before you go to a party, so you won't be so tempted to snack on chips." Women treat chips like they treat hard drugs. "I have one, and then I just can't control myself." Soon, we're making pace between the kitchen and the living room, just to grab another clandestine handful of sour-cream-and-onion chips. Soon, there will be a chip intervention, people tearfully crying, saying they found Pringles cans in your sock drawers.

It is always about the control. Fat, thin, chubby, or in between, you have to put an element of control into the way you're eating. My body isn't a temple; it's the security checkpoint at the airport. You can only carry 3.4 ounces or less of pasta and/or chicken.

It is a tradition passed on from the generations before me, along with yellowing *Family Circus* comics, decorative plates that say "just hand over the wine," and a million Bed Bath & Beyond coupons. My grandmother and aunts were dieting professionals since I was a kid. Even my mother, who is gracefully thin no matter how much she thinks otherwise, talks about the extra five pounds after Christmas like it's Rosemary's baby in her stomach, and not the delicious aftermath of cookies and eggnog and family time and happiness.

As a kid, nobody ever told me directly about dieting, but I heard things. The women in my life told me how beautiful I was. I heard that. I noticed how much all the women in my life wanted to change their own bodies. I heard people talking about it; I saw commercials; I saw that flimsy tabloid magazine at supermarket checkouts that was devoted just to pictures of women pulling out their jeans to show how much weight they had lost. I understood the endgame here. You were a work in progress, constantly. Extra weight was bad, but *ve haf our vays* of keeping it off.

Yogurt was one of those vays. Ah, yogurt. Yogurt is the kind of thing we're all told, nay, *forced*, to like. There was an ad campaign a few years ago in which these women would sit on chairs and kind of sexually moan over yogurt. I can confidently say I have never moaned over yogurt, sexually or otherwise. It is fine, but it's also very mucous-y. But there they were— commercials of women reaching their sexual peak over strawberry-cheesecake yogurt that tastes like the real thing, if the real thing were put in a blender and scolded till it lost all its fun.

Through conversations at Thanksgiving and Easter, talk shows, and the magazines lying around the house, I began to learn the *Good Housekeeping* mantras of dieting. These tricks are as old as humans themselves. There is a magazine cover featuring a low-fat whipped topping and Joan Lunden smeared in blood on the cave walls of our ancestors, no doubt.

I kept these tips and tricks in part of my brain as "things I knew I would need when I was older," along with minimal advice on taxes. I knew I would need these tips someday. Women diet. It's just what they do.

The basic commandments of dieting usually stay the same. Swapping, for instance. When dieting, I swapped everything I ate. I swapped potato chips for rice cakes. I swapped ice cream for fro-yo. Butter for olive oil. I swapped the real happiness of gooey for steamed. Or giant pots of beans, fresh vegetables, all with less salt and more pepper. Like I said, we all know how to diet.

I had been on diets since I was a teenager, both before and after my eating disorder. Usually, either I wanted to lose some amount or I wanted time to be erased from my body—like the September "I need to get off that summer weight" feeling, for example. The only thing that changed, however, was the fad diets. Oh, the fad diets. Fad diets are like Internet spam comments that tell you how much money people make per year working from home. We know they are fake, but sometimes, we just want to believe them.

When I was in high school, everything was low calorie or no calories. You counted all your calories and that was how you lost weight. Instead of eating low-calorie foods made low calorie by nature, you supplemented them with fake aspartame foods that were made low calorie by unreadable ingredients. That was the thing: you could eat anything you wanted, as long as it had been ruined by science or Snackwell's or Lean Cuisine. Or you could eat celery, which apparently made you lose weight while you chewed. Everything else was packaged, but at least you could eat macaroni and cheese, even if it tasted like somebody had run a hose over it.

To do this particular low-cal diet, you picked a food that existed and was delicious. Food science doctors would take it away from you, add chemicals to it, reduce the calories, and return it lifeless and disgusting. None of the food tasted like the thing it was supposed to, but I fooled myself because I was allowed to sometimes eat ice cream sandwiches. I also had to keep a "FOOD LOG" so I could count how many calories I had consumed, but honestly I lied so much about this it was pointless. In my FOOD LOG I mostly skipped how much butter I used. In my FOOD LOG I forgot to mention that I had snuck a couple of handfuls of shredded cheese. In my FOOD LOG I left out anything I ate standing up, like spoonfuls of Cool Whip or rice cakes I had sprayed with that neon yellow butter spray.

I also ate a veritable truckload of Lean Cuisines. I can't believe I did this. Back in high school, there were large freezer aisles full of Lean Cuisines devoted to every food and you had to eat them because they took up most of the grocery store. Now, the aisles with Lean Cuisines are much smaller because everybody, I think, ate Lean Cuisines and realized they would rather eat sewage. Have you ever had Lean Cuisine fettuccine Alfredo? It's like eating a hot cereal of instant milk and noodles made with piles of construction paper. Do you remember the Red Points? I am not talking about Hogwarts house points—I am talking about eating Swedish "meatballs" you heated up in your microwave and you got points for doing it. Once you got enough points, you received the worst prize ever, which was to stop eating for the day.

And you could get absolutely everything in those little one-hundred-calorie packs that I hoarded and consumed like a squirrel. My mouth was often stuffed with those wafer-thin crisps of Chips Ahoy! that tasted like you licked the floor. There were Pringles, animal crackers, any delicious thing would be ruined and replaced with horrible-tasting dirt. I would open up a package, take a bite, thinking *well, it says Cheez-It on this package so this will be a treat*, and do you remember that movie trailer with Angelina Jolie in it where she saw that kid and started screaming, "THAT'S NOT MY SON!!" I felt like that, I guess.

Then, there were the ZERO-calorie things. One time, I poured zero-calorie salad dressing on my car and it went through the paint. It invaded my brain until my parents screamed, "You are different" to me when my room became a sticky pod that communicated with my home planet.

I think the low-calorie diets sort of stemmed from the belief that women don't deserve to eat real food. I'm kidding about this, but only slightly. Like, what if they eat all the things they enjoy? What would they eat next??? *DOGS?! People?!*

I do think that this fad eventually died out because it was killing us, with all the chemicals. And the farther we got away from the eighties, the farther we got from the idea that you could snort chemicals up your nose and down your face and still live a functioning life. And the big lesson we all learned was that strict calorie counting our "food" wasn't the best way to lose weight, and also we were probably rotting our insides.

Once I was done with the low-cal thing, lest I fill my stomach with aluminum, I tried a variety of diets that did various forms of "it works, but then you gain the weight back when you eat like a human again." I tried to eat Special K cereal for two meals, which I believe went unsuccessfully because I ate three bowls for each meal with a gallon of whole milk at a shot. I tried to eat half a grapefruit with every meal. I tried to eliminate carbs, but found it impossible to do when I realized that pizza, of all things, is a carb! Didn't somebody declare that a salad?

But nothing, absolutely NOTHING beats the juice fast. If hell is real, the devil hands out green juice the moment you get in the door. You think it's not that bad, until you find yourself unable to poop for all of eternity and you start biting your nails just to chew on something solid.

I had a fine relationship with juice as a child. I obediently drank out of all the sippy cups of my youth. When I graduated from sippy cups to regular cups, I saw juice occasionally at continental breakfasts and whenever gin was around but tonic was not. It was sort of an afterthought for me. I thought about juice the way I thought about old episodes of *The King of Queens*. Fine when it was there, wouldn't go out of my way for it, doubted a return of its relevance.

Then, Los Angeles ruined everything. For a while, Los Angeles and New York City were like yin and yang. You would go to Los Angeles to wear colorful exercise gear and eat local organic and be on television, and you would go to New York to wear no colors at all, spend a lot of money on rent in order to be murdered, and eat more cream cheese than bagel. Then, we all started swapping spit on trends so the people in each city could get rid of their FOMO and also become know-it-alls on everything. New York started getting raw food/smoothie/ espresso bars. I would hear my West Coast friends talk about kale or acai bowls, and I would say, "Okay, in like seven months this is going to be in New York and I am going to hate it." Don't get me wrong. New York sends over plenty of trends to the West Coast: SoulCycle, brick-oven pizza, and overcharging for everything, but like New York City itself, the trends are always a little bit naughtier than the trends in LA. LA always sends over its guilt-ridden health trends. And LA couldn't have done us more wrong than with the damn juice.

Out of nowhere, I woke up in Brooklyn and juicing was a thing. One day, one of my friends is drinking a bloodred beet thing, and I make a topical *True Blood* joke, and boom! *True Blood* is lame and juice is everywhere. Nobody's regular anymore, and everybody in New York City becomes a little unhappier under the guise of "I've never felt better in my entire life."

Juice is basically this: imagine buying about twelve cents' worth of vegetables and then putting them in a blender and charging twelve bucks for them. That is juice. Again, this apparently makes you feel fantastic. Everybody tells me how fantastic they feel with all this juice. Everybody talks about getting rid of toxins like they don't have livers.

I mean, I get it. Vegetables are obviously healthy, and drinking a green juice after a hangover adds enough nutrients to my body to make me feel both healthy AND smug about my life. But then, somebody said, "Hey, if I feel good after one juice maybe I should drink juice for three days straight, lose a bunch of water weight, and make everybody in the whole world try this after me." And soon? The juice fast became trendy and appealed enough to my dieting sensibilities to warrant my trying it.

In the summer of 2012, my best friend and I went temporarily insane enough to try out a juice fast. It's not like living in New York City in ninety-five-degree weather isn't torturous enough: all the boroughs smell like garbage. The subway is similar to riding in a slightly air-conditioned armpit. You are a worthless vessel of sweat and "is this soaking wet tank top work-appropriate?" Everybody's already grumpy if it's not a weekend and they're not at a beer garden or on a beach.

But the beach, ah, the beach always beckoned. Summer is full of gluttony and high-calorie cocktails, but you have to look "bikini ready" at all times. Bikinis weren't just a functionally attractive item you could slap on and go to the beach wearing; you had to be bikini *ready* for them. Essentially, this meant you had to look like a swimsuit model, all flat stomach and no body hair, but do you know how hard that is for an average thin-curvy-sometimes-chubbyish person like me? Do you know how many women and people in general fluctuate on the body spectrum and consistently look far from "perfect"? Do you know how hard it is for a normal human being, such as myself, to look *fine* in a bathing suit? I'm not talking like "whoa, she fine," I'm talking "FINE in a retro tankini." I'll tell you: it's impossible. I have cellulite. I have that little bit of fat that bulges out between my breasts and my armpits. It's not like I am sitting on the couch like a giant slug, refusing to move until somebody pours salt on me. I MOVE. I am a living, breathing person who puts vegetables into herself and guess what? I like going to the beach. So what does one wear? A bathing suit. Fuck it. I might look my best in dark lips and a sexy gigantic T-shirt, but I gotta feed my calling to the sea.

And with juicing you could totally lose, like, five pounds in three days!

When we started our juicing expedition, going into the grocery store was probably very similar to getting married to Henry VIII. We were so excited and had no idea how horrible our lives were about to turn. We bought the required ingredients for the four different juices we would have over the course of three days: a tomato-based avocado thing, a berry/spinach combo, the master cleanse, and an almond-milk-dessert kinda deal.

Surely, you've heard of The Master Cleanse. It's a mix of

lemon juice, cayenne, maple syrup, and water. You drink it and become very thin and you probably hallucinate from hunger and lack of nutrients. Beyoncé did it for an extraordinary amount of time and to this day I have no idea why any of us do any of the things Beyoncé does because she is clearly on a different plane of existence than the rest of humanity. Try as I might, doing the things Beyoncé might do (naming my child after a plant or color, doing that hand thing to "Single Ladies," singing about paying bills), I would never be close to her.

So my best friend and I brought out our blender (juicers are expensive) and we drank six juices a day for three days. I stole the recipes off a juice bottle that cost about five times our daily budget.

I can remember it like it was yesterday. She and I would stand in the kitchen, the heat swirling around us, while I threw handfuls of spinach and dark berries into a small blender my mother had given us when we moved into the apartment. The mixture tasted fine, really, but put us into such a tailspin kind of focus that all we could think about was food: what we were eating and what we weren't.

"Is that enough? Is it done? Should we make more?"

For three days, we drank the juices, and *only* the juices. I dreamt about crackers. I dreamt about cracker crumbs. I dreamt about pizza and cookies, much like I usually did, but feeling more like a zombie thinking about brains. I found myself unable to focus on anything else. My friend and I would come home from work and lie on our futon, frantically drinking almond milk until we thought it was late enough to sleep. There, I could dream about going to bistros and gorging myself on real, chewable food. Our third roommate stayed at his boyfriend's house because he was so scared of us.

I had read that cleanses cleared toxins from the body, but

frankly I felt like the toxins were moving to my brain. I'd never felt angrier. I was, like, Winona Ryder in *Heathers* angry. Or quite honestly, Christian Slater in *Heathers* angry.

When I went off the diet, I lost around four pounds of water weight and half of my mind. I was inspired to eat healthily for a while after that, but mostly I forgot about it and kept on life as usual. Except! To this day, I still go on these juice fasts. No matter how much I was tortured from them, I still go on them. I've done them maybe two or three times since then, which is insane, because they do nothing but restrict you and make you feel like shit. But ah, isn't that just a diet?

I was in a wedding recently, and a couple of weeks before the wedding, I went on another juice fast. I wanted to drop pounds quickly and look good for pictures, and I knew it was the easiest way to do so. I restricted alcohol, carbs, dairy, meat, fun, refined sugar, joy. It was horrible. Of course it worked. I think the reason why I like juice diets so much is because they get down to the bare bones of what it usually means to be on a diet. There's no pretense. All food is bad. No guilt, no slipups, no cheat days: just absolute, regimented vegetable nothingness. It felt like torture because it was. It felt like starvation and deprivation because it was.

But isn't that what I've been doing my entire life? Low-calorie foods, egg whites, juice? Isn't it all the same thing when you feel bad?

I've spent my entire life fighting food. I've spent years feeling guilty about it. I can tell you it's not even to look a certain way, anymore. I like the idea of "seeing" results, but my body has been on the same roller-coaster ride for a long time—gaining ten pounds by eating with absolute reckless abandon, losing ten pounds, gaining it again, restricting myself, and the cycle repeats. I wouldn't know what to do if that wasn't my life. I wouldn't know how to act or eat if I wasn't on one of those peaks. If I was being naughty, or if I was being good.

I believe that, most of the time, we are on diets because it's considered taboo *not* to be. We are supposed to be constant works in progress, never satisfied, never able to achieve the GOAL WEIGHT, always striving for it. Can you imagine a woman you know saying something like "Oh, no, I'm 100 percent happy with my body. Not a thing I would change. Nope, not *one thing*"? How fucking quickly do you think somebody at the table would say, later on, "Her thighs are actually a little big"?

We are *all* critics of the female figure. I have heard the things men say about bathing suit pictures they're viewing on Facebook. I have heard women talk about their friends when they've gone to the bathroom. So, to combat that, we become "self-aware" of our flaws by saying we're on a diet, by watching what we eat, by saying, "I know I need to lose that extra flab." We diet to combat the hate, to defend ourselves from comments, in the hopes that people know at least we are trying to fix ourselves. That we're improving.

Being healthy or getting in shape aren't bad things. I just believe you can love your body as is, even when you are in the process of changing it. I believe you can do this by changing the desire from "wanting to lose weight" to "wanting to gain power, strength, and health." The power we can get from the power we give to our bodies is a fantastic thing. But healthy people don't *deprive* themselves of anything. Why deprive yourself when you can give yourself so much? *Give* yourself strength and stamina through exercise; *give* yourself nutrients and vitamins by eating well.

And I love eating healthy. The truth is, I actually find salmon kind of delicious. If you blacken it with some good seasoning and serve it with a nice side salad of arugula with lemon and olive oil, it's pretty satisfying. I love delicious, creamy avocado, with all its healthy fats and vitamins. I love mincing garlic and baking tofu and roasting chickpeas. I love walking through the farmer's market and choosing a rainbow of delicious fruits and vegetables—purple spicy radishes, pickled beets, spiced carrots, red and green Swiss chard, white jicama. I love eating whole grains and quinoa and barley, loaded with olive oil and fresh herbs.

Here's the other thing. After years of fighting, and depriving, and holding back, I realized something important about myself: I love food. There is something inside of me, something raw and animalistic, that sees a plate of nachos and wants to house the entire thing. I love food-truck fare and processed cheese and hot dogs at baseball games. I love shoving my face into an entire hamburger or drunkenly making myself a grilled cheese. I love butter. I love it all—from the high-end, expensive fusion cuisine to the ninety-nine-cent bags of Cheetos, to the trendy dumplings and artisanal gelato, all the way down to hastily boiled ramen noodles, I love food.

I am well aware that if I practiced restraint and ate only grilled chicken and egg whites and raw kale that I would have the body I really thought I wanted. If I worked out religiously, joined a gym, woke up at six a.m., drank green juice, and started my day off right, I would look exactly as I imagine when I fantasize about slipping into a tight black dress or an impossibly fresh outfit.

However, I've come to realize something, and it's a radical thing for me: I am not willing to sacrifice my joy of food to be thin. I will never be thin unless I make a conscious effort to do so. I am genetically curvy, or chubby if you want to say chubby, with a fat tummy and cellulite thighs and arms that jiggle a bit. I also have thin, long legs, a larger chest, and a thin face. Without a consistent, persistent exercise regimen and a restricted, mostly healthy diet, that is the kind of body I will have.

I can't give up delicious things, and I don't want to, and I'm much happier when I don't. I want to treat myself on a consistent basis, and don't want to get up early every morning to work out. So, instead of desiring to be thin when I don't want to put the work in, I will happily learn to love my body, treat it properly, and reward it with delicious horrible crap when I so desire.

I know all the rules of diet and exercise. I have chosen a balance for myself that works for me, to keep me sane and happy. I exercise infrequently, but still put in the time to run or go to spin-cycle class or take long walks at least once or twice a week. I walk instead of taking the subway whenever possible. I eat healthy more than I eat unhealthy, and I try to cook my meals at home and limit salt and oil consumption. My general rule is this: if I don't crave the bad food, I don't eat it. I don't grab a slice of pizza or order takeout because it's easier than cracking an egg and whipping up an omelet. I treat myself to something I love a couple of times a week. I don't turn down potato chips, but I always keep fresh veggies in my fridge.

On occasion, I decrease my unhealthy food and increase the juice, the vegetables, and running habits. I work out a little more and eat a little less junk. And I lose a couple of pounds until whatever event I wanted to look good at happens, or whatever dress I wanted to look cute in is worn, and then I go back to normal.

Maybe one day I will change. For now, I will live my life with greens in my belly and a little bit of back fat. I choose to live with the freedom of my own choices, and I refuse to guilt myself or shame myself for them.

I will find balance. I will stop using the word "diet." And I will stop feeling so bad about myself. Swim against the current for a change. And you should, too.

Believe me, the salmon will thank you.

Sex Ed for Young Women

Hello, and welcome to Sex Ed for Young Women. What do *I* know about sex? That's a good question, and so I'm glad I asked it. I have been having sex for about a decade now, so I know very, very little. I know that sex has an odd, lingering smell that permeates your bedsheets. I know that smell isn't *necessarily* sinful. I know that thinking about sex either turns me on or makes me very tired. I know how many fingers one should use during "let's just do it and then watch an episode of *Justified*" weeknight intercourse, during "we've had two glasses of whiskey each, which is *just enough*" weekend-relationship sex, and during "I will never, ever see you again because I hate you, but goddamn are you sexy" single-person sex. I know that sex feels like jelly, if jelly could scream.

This was all learned through trial, a lot of error, and a little research. I am certainly not what one would call a "sexpert," which I believe is shorthand for "surprise him by wearing a tie, and only a tie" or "put an ice cube in your mouth and go down on someone." While an expert I am not, from the moment I stopped being a virgin, I have had to wade through a bunch of sticky slime to learn what few things I know now, and that's not just a euphemism because bars are *also* very sticky.

I was formally taught about sex twice. That's it. Two lessons and then I was sent off and running, trying to figure out the specific part you can push on my body to make it feel better than it usually does when it's just sitting and relaxing.

The first time I took a sex-education class was in fifth grade. Our parents had to sign a note that said it was okay to be in the elementary school sex class, which is a very polite way of asking, "How religious *are* you?" My brother had brought this slip home a few years earlier. My mother signed it willingly, but insisted he learn what sex was like from ole Mom and Dad first, lest he go in totally unaware and start screaming. This was public school, after all. They could have handed us a copy of *The Scarlet Letter* or a xeroxed sheet of the Kama Sutra and called it a day for all she knew. My dad brought my brother up into my parents' bedroom for a "chat" and my brother came out looking nervous and a little smarter.

Up until fifth grade, I was completely and blissfully unaware of what sex actually was. Kids had way less access to the Internet than they do now, so the only information you could garner was secondhand from other children, and other children are wrong and stupid. Either way, I had gathered some evidence and had my suspicions. My brother, who was a child lunatic, told me that you could get pregnant if you fell asleep on a pillow with a cartoon character on it, especially if you kissed it when you were sleeping. I knew that sex was kissing. I also knew that sex was kissing to *music*, because my mother always used to cover my face when people on television began to heavily make out to slow music. I absolutely knew that a lot of kissing was involved, and in this way I was right. Kissing is about 33 percent of sex, maybe about 60 percent of sex in college, and 0 percent if you are Julia Roberts in *Pretty Woman* before she met Richard Gere. I also figured that sex was kissing naked, because that is what kids who walked in on their parents said. Oh! And the whole thing was only physically possible to do if you loved each other very, very much. So I had some leads in this area.

When it was time for me to bring the sheet to my parents, my mother signed it willingly. I waited to be led into a room and come out smarter, after my parents had given me a cool spoiler alert about the whole thing. Instead, my mother told me what heterosexual sex was when I was in the shower, the night before the class, while she was sitting outside it. I'll tell you one thing: I had not considered this combination of body parts *at all.* I was completely blown away. I would never let any man stick his pee machine *inside of me*, which is gross sounding because it *is gross. No, thank you. Hard pass.*

The next day, in the class, the instructors separated the girls from the boys. I remember the class started with an exercise: we had to say "penis" and "vagina" out loud to each other until we stopped giggling. The teacher just kept yelling, "Stop laughing!" which are the two magic words to make people laugh, and to this day, we're still stunted little fifth graders who laugh at the word "penis."

I also remember how very serious the class was. A large diagram of a uterus was shown on the projector. You know, that classic diagram that looks like a kraken, or the Alien from *Alien*, which was still popular at the time. This is what most girls look like on the inside. Why? *Because deep inside, all little girls are monsters!* Just kidding. It's because we have to squeeze little babies out of us! The teacher tells us that we all look like this because our bodies are little baby factories that pop out children when we are older. We are the factories. The boys are the factory workers. Do you get it? When we are older, the eggs in our stomachs grow to be the humans we are today. Does it sound fun? It isn't! It's very serious. *Now say "penis" again.*

I felt vaguely uncomfortable with this idea. I had *never* believed in the stork. If the stork was so busy giving every human in the world a baby, why did he also need to moonlight as a pickle salesman? The numbers just didn't add up, and also I had seen *The Birds* by Alfred Hitchcock and trusted NO BIRD. Still, when my mother said "make a baby" in reference to sex, it hadn't completely computed. I just figured you did it, and like a pager or one of those light-up discs you get while waiting at an Olive Garden, you would just have to wait a small period of time and then get what you want. When I realized that this was all on me, I was annoyed. I never wanted to *do* anything. I never wanted to carry anything for anybody. All I wanted to do was watch cartoons and eat. Still, it seemed like it was my responsibility to house the children, much like people were forced to house American soldiers during the Revolutionary War, which we were learning about at the time.

The little boys came filing back into the classroom, looking a little bit different and a little bit stoked. The girls? Not stoked. All different. No smiles from the girls, and you know why—we were just handed the burden of womanhood, at age ten. I couldn't even handle a large backpack.

From that point on, I grew up thinking sex was very disgusting and very technical, and mostly, all on me.

When I was twelve years old, I remember being with my mother on a trip to the grocery store. I announced a plan: I would not have sex for a long time, if at all, on account of how gross it is. My mother responded with the stock parenting answer: "When you're in love, you'll want to." While I was already vaguely in love with a couple of celebrities, including Greg Brady, I knew she meant something a little deeper.

The next time we had to take sex education in public school was in high school, when I was around fifteen years old. This time, I found myself very interested in boys, and suddenly very uninterested in my previous declarations of celibacy. At this age, we were pretty aware of what sex *was*. We were all comfortable with the fact that ladies could, given the opportunity, squeeze babies out of themselves. I already had a very scarring first period, on the first day of seventh grade. I knew my body could betray me for the sake of womanhood at any given moment. However, sometime around this time we learned another pivotal point about sex: people had sex because they enjoyed it. We knew this through a variety of different bad influences. Older people we eavesdropped on. Television. Movies. We also knew this because, now, we were old enough to be attracted to people, and our bodies felt like they were *on fucking fire. Nobody let us know that we would feel like we were on fire.*

I was at the point in my life when I wasn't so sure I wanted to have sex, but I was *very* sure I wanted to heavily make out with any boy who came within two feet of me. It was confusing. It was hormonal. It was thrilling and also horrible. I had a crush on a different boy each week in an ever-increasing and frantic manner. I wanted to make out with Ben Affleck, Shawn Hunter, every man on the ABC TGIF lineup, two of my teachers, some of my brother's friends, the cute deli boy at Stop & Shop, and the pizza boy. I was also very much *in love* with the most popular boy in school, who one time fed me a French fry and drove me to Stew Leonard's. To him, I devoted all my late-night sing-alongs to Kelly Clarkson, Coldplay, and My Chemical Romance. Same kinda longing, expressed in very different manners.

Instead of addressing these budding feelings, the class taught us about the birth canal. Again, the boys were separated from the girls. I think the most *unique* thing about my high school sexual-education class was who taught it. Imagine you are a fifteen-year-old girl who is confused about her growing sexual feelings. Now, imagine you are going to take a class that will fill an educational requirement and also hopefully shed light on some of your questions. Great. Now, imagine learning the answers from your giant gym teacher. I want you to add a large, almost vintage mustache on this gym teacher. I want you to add the kind of khaki shorts that were, in a way, too short for an adult male. I want you to imagine learning about sex from a man who looked like steroided-up Mr. Holland of *Mr. Holland's Opus* fame. I want you to imagine this man speaking the way Mr. T spoke when he taught high school wrestling.

Now, I wonder, are you going to ask him any questions?! Are you going to say to him, "Hey, I'm a teenager and I'm having this sexual awakening, and I'm not sure how to rationally explain it, and I'm also a little nervous"?

No? You're going to sit in the back of the class and try to never look him in the face again? Okay. Great.

One of the things I remember being taught in that class was that sex is very dangerous. I know this is portrayed in the movie *Mean Girls*, so it seems like it may have been done for comic relief, but nope. Public school sex education put the fear of death into our hearts. We learned the myriad of ways in which one could physically die from sex. It could be from childbirth, which still rings as true today as it did in medieval times. It could be from untreated sexually transmitted infections. STIs were everywhere, but they were mostly at parties.

Everyone we were attracted to had loads of them, which would cause sores all over our bodies and eventually kill us the way vampires were killed by the sun.

Then, we watched the video.

You know exactly what video I am talking about. It was the grainy film about birth, which starred a British lady, her pregnant stomach, and her outstanding pubic hair. Ah, the pubic hair that looked like the very hairy baby head crowning, until you actually saw the baby crowning, and then you wanted to throw up because it seemed so painful and no reasonable human should do it at all. It was a *Scared Straight!* tactic. Of course, we already had a feeling it was painful. Our mothers cryptically alluded to this pain all the time, so you had a reasonable understanding of it. *It was so rewarding, I forgot about the pain*, is basically how Braveheart reasoned being pulled from limb to limb and gutted so he could reunite with his wife. We knew it hurt. But to see it on a tiny thirty-two-inch television screen on VHS? I don't know a better way to put this. It was a real fuckin' boner killer. Nobody in his or her right mind wanted to have sex after that. We were scarred.

The only other sex-education lessons we got during those sessions were given rushed. If you have sex, the gym teacher said, even though nobody wanted our gym teacher to give us sex advice, use a condom. That's it. No "it's going to be really uncomfortable and he's not going to know how to put the condom on." No "the condom is going to ruin the moment when he *puts* the condom on." Nothing. Just that condoms were available, and if you wanted to be super safe and alive, you could "heavy pet," which meant dry humping, which most of us had already figured out in the back of cars after homecoming. That was about it. Again, the boys came back stoked and the girls came back . . . different. We knew what could happen to us if things went wrong. We could have a child rip through our almost presidential bush of pubic hair. Men just became carriers for HPV, which had fewer consequences for men than being late for a dinner reservation.

That was all the sex education I had: the penis goes in the vagina, and if you have sex when you're young, you have to be careful or a baby comes flying out of your pubes. I believe these are important lessons to start off with. I believe children should learn basic anatomy. I believe children should learn to use condoms and how a baby is made. In fact, a lot of children aren't even taught *that*. They are taught abstinence education, which is (a) proven not to work and (b) of *course it doesn't work.* If I didn't know what condoms were before I had sex for the first time, I wouldn't have "not had sex," I would have "not used a condom." For Christ's sake, do you know how resistant teenagers are to using condoms to begin with?

But besides giving these lessons, we should fill in some of those confusing blanks, too. For one thing, sexual education shouldn't be so heterosexual and cisgender (which, if you don't know, means you feel you are the gender you were assigned at birth) oriented. If you're queer, you're going to hear "the penis goes into the vagina" and say, "Nah, what else?" and then be met with radio silence. If you're transgender, you're *only* taught that "women have vaginas and make babies and men have the baby sticks," and that's not entirely true for everyone either. We need to be taught at a young age that some of us have different desires, different parts, and a lot of *different everything.* Teenagehood is the time we are all busting at the seams to figure out who we are and what kind of sex we might be interested in having. Now's the time to explain the options. We also need to talk about sex in a way that acknowledges teenagers are actually interested in having sex, instead of pretending they are Christian cartoon characters. And mostly, and I cannot stress this enough, we need to learn one of the most important things about sex of all time. We need to learn it with all the boys and all the girls in one room, together:

Consent.

Never once was I taught about sexual consent, and that you have the option of saying *no* to sex. Never once did I hear about boys learning that they aren't entitled to sex, or that they have the option of saying no to sex, too. It is as important as safe sex, because it *is safe sex*.

Why teach this young? Because that's all we get. Because everything after that is through word of mouth, the Internet, porn, peer pressure, and how society handles sex. Society has long been a fan of boys being sexual, horny, dominating beings and women being meek. Society has long favored boys having more access to knowledge because they are allowed to talk about sex more frequently, and with more detail. Society likes it straight and graphic on television, but straight and reserved in real life.

After those classes, I learned about sex in cars and at parties. I didn't know what was normal for a sexually active woman. I knew that men had wet dreams and woke up with boners, and we had to hear on repeat how this was totally normal and it's okay and a regular thing. But I didn't know I could masturbate, too. I didn't know I would have weird feelings and weird dreams, too. I had to practically beg my friend to let me know what a blow job was. She showed me what it was like on the stick shift of a car. I didn't know the importance of an orgasm, but I knew the importance of faking it. I knew I shouldn't have sex with too many people or I'd be considered a slut, but I didn't know how to find the nearest Planned Parenthood, or the different kinds of birth control I could use to protect myself. I had practically no information at all, beyond the bare bones of sex. It took me a really long time to fill those blanks in.

That's why I'm here! I'm here to fill in those pesky blanks in case they were never filled in for you, using the little knowledge I have about having sex as a woman. Welcome to my Sexual Education, Ladies.

Virginity Isn't a Big Deal
(We're Starting Off Strong, Here)

When I was seventeen, I stopped being a virgin.

I stopped being a virgin because I had what I considered to be sexual intercourse for the first time.

Wait! Let me jump in with another lesson: **Sticking a penis in a vagina isn't the only definition of sex.**

I know this feels weird and hippie dippie and like I'm a sixty-year-old San Francisco mom about to sit you down and tell you weird stories about LSD and the body and all my orgies. But hear me out: we have a very weird obsession with defining what kind of sex you are having, and it's not always necessary.

When you spend the night with a cute young thing and afterward people ask, "Hey, did you guys hook up?" and you say yes, people want even more info. They want you to delve very deeply into what digits you used, whether the mouth was involved, and all that jazz. It feels kind of weird, like you have to legitimize with people that the sexy acts you were doing were valid enough to qualify as sex. There's also the really irritating thing people do when they ask lesbians what "sex is for them." There are also the people whom you have never had sex with but "did stuff with" whom you still felt an emotional connection to. All it means is that the idea of "sex" is allowed to have some leeway. Sex doesn't always have to mean "a penis enters you." We don't need a penis for non-baby-producing sex! I'm not saying this in a way that makes me against penises. I'm heartily for them at the right time. I just don't think that the act of some dude sticking his schlong into you has to be the *only* definition of sex we keep in our dictionary. You don't have to validate your actions or your sex life for anyone.

Okay! Back to our regularly scheduled programming.

Back to Why Virginity Isn't a Big Deal

I did not lose my virginity. I know exactly where it went. It went on top of a futon in a basement that you could enter through a sliding door. Nobody took my virginity, because my virginity wasn't a landmass that Columbus entered and then ruined. Nobody *took* my virginity, because my virginity wasn't a number-two pencil somebody asked to borrow during a Scantron test and never gave back. Nobody *took* my virginity at all. I had sex for the first time in a condo with a sarcastic dude whom I sort of liked. I don't feel like this is a sad story.

When I was seventeen, I stopped being a virgin because I no longer saw fit to be a virgin anymore. Nine years later, this fact does not affect my life. It was not the foundation that built my relationships for the future. The loss of my virginity was not a memory viewed from a Vaseline-blurred lens that I replay in my mind like a Nicholas Sparks novel-turned-movie. The act lasted about four minutes, and it was fine. It was consensual and it was safe, and years later I had sex with somebody who really meant something to me. I took more out of that kind of love than I ever did with my first time.

As a woman, I know this is an odd thing to say. I am aware that my very *preciousness* as a woman is built on the notion that my virginity is a flower. I am aware that virginity is clothed in white nightgowns that ripple in the wind. I am aware that sex and innocence are so tightly wound for women you could French braid them. I am aware that I was supposed to one day lovingly hand this flower to an important man. You know, like the way Arwen handed back the necklace in *The Lord of the Rings*. I know that my virginity was prized. I know all this. I just don't *care* about it. Some people do, and that's nice, too. I just don't.

When people asked me what my "first time" was like with wide, curious eyes, I replied, "Well, it was *fine*." They'd ask me if it was with my first boyfriend, or a great love, and I would say no. Then they would ask if he was a great friend, and I would say, "He was a very nice guy." When they looked sad for me, I felt bad. I amped up the story with little details, like how much he made me laugh and how *cool* he was about the whole thing. "There," I thought. "That's better."

I do not consider myself precious. I do not consider my virginity to be a budding rose. I consider it to be the first action in a series of actions I would do again, with less worthy and more worthy people. Oh sure, I cared about it at that time. I was seventeen. Attention was paid to it. I think about it in the way that I think of most of the things I did when I was seventeen years old: *Eh. I feel differently now.*

Having sex for the first time is certainly a monumental decision, in the sense that you have to make sure you are emotionally ready and you are old enough to be rational (and legal) and you are sound of mind enough to be safe. Use protection.

Be ready. You don't have to be totally in love, unless you are. You don't have to think of sex as losing your innocence. You aren't losing anything.

You are gaining experience. Be ready for that experience, and you will be just fine.

Sex Isn't Dirty

Every girl is terrified of being labeled a whore. It can really sully a reputation. The way you get to be called a whore? Well, sometimes it's sex. Sometimes it's just because people don't like you, or because they think you flirt too much, or they think you wear tight clothing. Whatever reason you are called a whore, the definition remains the same for women across the board. It means you are less worthy as a human being because people are not comfortable with the way you choose to express your sexuality. I'm not sure how sexual you have to be to be considered a whore. Well, I kind of do. It's any hint of sexual energy at all. Just show any hint, any trace, any microscopic evidence of having feelings of a sexual nature. You'd have to be a character in a Laura Ingalls Wilder book not to be considered a whore. You have to be a snail not to be considered a whore. The scale is pretty objective, always changing, and impossible to predict. Basically, if you are a woman, somebody has probably considered you a whore at one point in your life.

Great!

Guys never get called whores. They get called heartbreakers, or Casanovas, or bachelors. They are off the hook for this one. This is nuts, because if we're in the business of calling people whores in the first place, because if we called anybody *in the world that*, it would be Robin Thicke. I am saying this in case this book is wildly successful, because I want this on record: I think Robin Thicke should be flushed down the toilet.

Anyway. A woman's purity is very closely tied with her sexual history. Have sex with too many people, and you are no longer pure. I do not know what this magic number is at all. I'm officially asking, by the way. What is the appropriate amount of sex you can have before somebody considers you a whore? What's too much? What's too little? I'd like to know. After all these years my friends and I have been devalued for our sexual decisions, I want to know the exact constraints and guidelines of how not to be a whore. If the number is zero, why is it not zero for a man? If the number is one, or "waiting for marriage," why are you called a prude?

Right. Because there is no magic number. In fact, I'll give you a magic number. Infinity. The world is infinite. Have sex with as many people as you safely see fit.

Consensual sex isn't a dirty act and nobody has the right to make you feel bad about it. Choosing to have sex with whom you want is not a bad thing. You are entitled to have fun and to have sex. You are allowed to have flings, to get back with an ex-boyfriend for one night, to sleep with a woman because you want to, to try something with more than one person, and it doesn't mean you aren't smart or interesting or good.

Enjoy yourself, get tested, and run away from anyone who is concerned about the number of people you've had sex with. Or just answer with a classy, no-fail response:

"After your family reunion, I kind of lost count."

Masturbate

The first time I learned to masturbate was, perhaps, more fantastic and memorable to me than most sexual encounters.

I have to stress this: for many, many years I had no *idea* that women could masturbate. Men, they seemed to masturbate at the mere *idea* of human contact. It was as casual as khakis and mentioned as much as bathrooms, beef jerky, and hookups. Women: they never pooped, they smelled like roses, and they certainly never masturbated. That was a man thing. For years, I had never even considered it for myself.

Until:

I was nineteen and in *The City*. I didn't live there, yet. I was in the West Village, and the West Village at nineteen was nothing like it is today. Not because it *looked* different, but because it felt big and wild to me. Now? I walk around with the kind of seasoned indifference that people who live here fail to even realize. Then, they remember how bright the West Village used to feel, and how it still looks exactly the same (just with a lot more fro-yo shops).

I was with one of my best friends, Nat, who hailed from Oregon but felt more New York to me than anyone else. She came into places and left those places bigger than they were before. She was bright, cynical but bubbly, and most important, she could always get us drinks. We tucked into a West Village bistro that served us pizzas with chewy crusts and fresh herbs, that served us mussels and ciabatta and salads with goat cheese. And sangria. As much wine as I wanted. No ID. I went particularly wild, just to feel the words "more wine, please" on my tongue. Nat introduced me to Marie and Lauren, two girls who were sexy without even trying. We were talking the way women do when they are full and drunk and happy and young. In other words, we were talking about sex.

Marie mentioned something about masturbation, because she was in a dry spell and at least she had her vibrator. I said, smugly, "Well, I don't masturbate."

I certainly felt this was a good thing. I was nineteen and still trying very hard to discover my identity. At this point it was Gothic and Abstinent, with dyed black hair and tight black dresses, who abstained from everything (but wine) in a way that made me feel superior and enlightened.

"What do you *mean*, you don't masturbate?"

Nobody needs to answer this kind of rhetoric, but I did anyway. I had never tried it because I doubted it would work, I explained. I had never tried it because I thought it was more of a guy thing, and women don't do it. Women didn't need to masturbate! They had to wait patiently until they could find someone to stick fleshy things into their holes. I waited my sexual urges out, letting them practically bubble over during Shonda Rhimes shows, then went to work feeling tightly wound, like a proper lady! I was speaking nonsense to deaf ears. It didn't matter what I said. Wine, mussels, and New York City had hatched a plan for my future, and it was the sex shop next door.

"No! You have to masturbate, and we have to get you a vibrator."

There wasn't much of a discussion, here. There was no debate. We paid our bill and passed three head shops, a tattoo parlor, and a Gray's Papaya. It felt like I was in an episode of *Taxicab: Confessions*.

The sex shop was brightly lit. I had never seen so many dildos in one room. More accurately, I had never seen one dildo in one room. It was exhausting. I wandered over to a tiny light blue penis.

"This seems fine."

They were not satisfied. They were about to teach me the ways of the independent clitoral stimulation, something which I had no experience with. They led me to the Pocket Rocket, a modest hot-pink vibrator that looked somewhat like a cosmetic tool. It was twenty dollars. There was to be no penetration involved. Just me, three AA batteries, and a night in. I doubted I would take any enjoyment out of this!

Up to this point, I hadn't had many orgasmic moments. I am not sure many college girls do. Sex wasn't a give-and-take; it was a give. I gave because it was what you did; it was how you kept relevant and modern and in touch with someone you felt a stirring for. Mostly, I enjoyed kissing and cuddling. I began to feel like I wasn't a sexual being, which I think is the great tragedy of not masturbating. Not taking this kind of stuff in your own hands, not allowing yourself to figure it out, can make you feel isolated from your own sexuality. Your sexual feelings come entirely from the moments you are having sex, so they become extremely dependent on the person you are doing it with. If that person doesn't give you what you want, you can't tell the person what you want because you don't really know yet, so you have bad sex, go home, and chalk up your sexual exploration to whatever other people have offered you. This is what masturbation is for. It's just you, what works for you, and whatever fantasies you didn't realize you could have.

I came home on Metro-North and retreated to my room. I put the television on because I needed to find something loud, and settled on the E! Entertainment network, which was trying out a reality show with Katie Price. I went under my covers.

Bliss. Fucking incredible bliss. It was bliss because I did it myself; it was bliss because it was under my control; it was bliss because I never thought it could be that good. From this, I began to learn the pace I liked, what buttons you could push, and how hard or how soft you should go on me. I began to grab hold of what I liked.

Masturbating led me to a very important path in my sexual history, which, in fact, is another lesson:

Explore. Find what works for you.

Once I started masturbating, I began to figure out the kinds of things I enjoyed about sex. When I said "harder," or "yes, yes" in the past, it was because I felt like it was something I had to say, or because the person I was with had accidentally stumbled on to something that felt good. I never could give anybody any real direction on this, unfortunately. The most dreaded question one of my partners could ask me was, *What do you like?* Uh, dude! I don't know! You're supposed to know! You're supposed to touch me and figure it out yourself! I don't fucking know! That's kind of nuts. It's not somebody else's job to figure out what you like in bed. You can figure it out together, maybe, but you should have some semblance of what you enjoy down there. It's a revolutionary feeling when you take your sexuality in your own hands, and you really deserve to do that.

I don't just mean exploring in ways people touch you. I want to stress how important it is for girls to explore *everything.* If you think you're interested in women, try it. If you read fan fiction about BDSM and it gets you all tingly, think about trying BDSM. If you think you're interested in *anything legal*, don't be afraid to try it. Life's short, man. Get a little weird with it.

On a side note, for me, life opened up a little with my

trusty Pocket Rocket. I figured out exactly the areas that worked for me, and I could give better directions to those places than I could the closest diner from my apartment. I had that Pocket Rocket for two years before I wore it out. It just cracked and died when I was visiting my parents. I was too afraid to throw it out in the tiny bathroom trash, though, so I kept the pieces in the back of my old American Girl doll dresser. I would take them with me to Boston, where I could throw them out in relative peace.

Of course, I forgot about them. Months later, I came home again and remembered they were there. I went to retrieve them.

They were gone.

I cannot *believe* we don't tell girls to masturbate. It really is the greatest. But on a personal note, I use my hands now. But that's because I always forget to buy batteries.

Oh, and while we are on that note of safety:

Use protection. All the time.

I don't care if he tells you it feels better without a condom and he can pull out. Use a fucking condom. I am telling you this and reiterating this because I know some schmuck is going to try to pull out, and he is going to tell you he is good at pulling out, and I heartily recommend going to a diner and getting cheese fries instead.

Lesson: Don't listen to anybody trying to convince you of anything.

Which, of course, brings me to shaving: **Shave as much as you like, and do what you feel comfortable with.**

I have no real qualms with pubic hair, as long as it is your preference. It's just that nobody should decide this for you. Shaving your pubic hair is really awful. It takes me almost thirty minutes in the shower, and then I have to wipe the whole shower down so my roommate doesn't have to take her next shower surrounded by my hair forest. I can't use regular shaving cream; I have to use the no-ingrown-hairs one so I don't look like I have some kind of sexual disease. The hair grows back immediately, and it's itchy, but somehow, through all of this, I like the look more. Of course, the big question is, do I like this because it looks better, or do I like this because society tells me it's what looks better? I grapple with this too often to have some dude tell me his preferences on the issue.

So, I settle with shaving sometimes, and then being way too lazy to ever do it in the winter. In the winter, a mild trim will do.

The point is, preferring a lot of pubic hair doesn't make having sex harder. If it is what you like, nobody should tell you that you are being unclean or ask you to shave. However, if you are seeing somebody you like and the person states a preference without any pressure to change, don't feel like you are killing feminism if you feel okay with a compromise. And, most important, if you like shaving your entire region, and somebody tells you that it's wrong because it makes you look like a baby, that person is a lunatic. You are an adult woman who happens to have no pubic hair. You are not a Lolita. You are an *adult woman*.

Groom as you fucking please.

Now, one more lesson:

You can say no to the kind of sex you don't want.

I want you to soak this in. I don't care if he's your boyfriend of ten years. I don't care if you started giving him a blow job and you decide you don't want to anymore. I don't care if you were drunk and flirting with him. I don't care if you want to stop now, after all that *work*. I don't care if you started feeling weird out of nowhere. Don't be afraid of what the person might think if you say no. Don't worry if he won't like you because of it, or get mad because of it. Say no if you get uncomfortable. Don't be afraid to say no. Consent is what makes sex enjoyable. Consent is what you deserve.

Tell the people you want to have sex with a resounding yes, and then enjoy the hell out of it, with no shame. Let it always start with a yes. You do not deserve to ever have sex that leaves you feeling like you should have said no.

That is the only rule of sex that should never, ever be broken.

Until next time, ladies, this has been Sex Ed for Young Women. Have fun out there, because sex should always be gross, smelly, and a hell of a lot of fun.

Does This Skirt Make
Me Look Feminist?

Imagine you are dancing to a song in a club. The song is by Nicki Minaj. Nicki Minaj is not only a talented rap queen; she is also a feminist. She has been known to make some beautifully feminist statements (look up her video comparing the different connotations of "bossed up" and "bitch") while not giving a hoot if you think her butt is real or not. I love her. This feels good. You are in a club, dancing with your friends, and you are still being a good feminist.

Boom. Chris Brown is on this verse? Motherfucking human slug *Chris Brown*? You have some options here. You can leave the dance floor, you can make a face and keep dancing, or you can stand on the table like Sally Field in *Norma Rae* holding a sign that says UNION until the DJ stops. You're a feminist! Which means, of course, that no matter the circumstances *you cannot screw this up*. If you do, the whole system collapses. Everything we've worked for up to now will be destroyed. There is no room for error, if you are a feminist! If you call your friend a bitch, or pick up a magazine in a waiting room that has an article about pleasing your man, or watch a movie that fails the Bechdel test, or stay silent when some jank from high school tweets a pro-choice status . . . what happens then? Are you a giant flaming hypocrite?

Uh, no. Don't worry. No.

I can't tell you how many times somebody has asked me, *Is it feminist to . . . ?*

Sometimes, this comes from a nice place—a genuine question that comes from the idea that in order to *be* a feminist and to call yourself a feminist, you have to have all the answers to feminism right away. Like that scene in *X-Men* in which Professor X puts on his little brain hat and then gets the knowledge of the entire world. Little brain hats that give you all the answers are an inaccurate portrayal of my feminism. Nobody has all the answers. You learn things as you go along. You are allowed to change your perceptions and opinions as you go along, too.

Sometimes, it comes from a place where people are trying to "catch you." When I told a male acquaintance that I was a feminist, his answer to me was, "So I guess that just totally excuses all the times you were drunk and dancing on tables, huh?" Well, first of all, I did that *once*, and I was also chucking ice cubes at couples who were showcasing too much PDA, so I feel like it evens out. Second of all, *so fucking what*?! Being a feminist doesn't mean being perfect, and it definitely doesn't mean you can't have fun.

Even if somebody isn't questioning me, I still worry at times that I am doing something *wrong*. I think that we all want to be good at feminism because we believe in it, and we don't want to contribute to anything that will prevent things from progressing. A lot of women ask feminists, "Is this feminist??" not because they are really scared of screwing up. It's mostly because these slipups always, always get broadcast and pointed out. It is a subtle way of tearing us down.

The feminist police are lurking in our Internet corners. They are ready to tear out your trachea if you so much as mention that dress codes should exist in schools even though they historically single out young women for being *distracting to boys*, like boys are animals that can't handle the sight of a bra strap. Beyoncé and Emma Watson declare they are feminists, and there's a million different think pieces about why they aren't, why they aren't good for the movement, and more. It wasn't until Roxane Gay declared herself a "bad feminist," that is, *a work in progress*, that people even acknowledged you can make mistakes and still have good intentions. You can fuck up and still believe in the social, political, and economic equality of the sexes. I danced to "Blurred Lines" at a recent wedding because my boyfriend's grandma wanted me to! I'm not saying it didn't slowly kill me inside, but I'm saying I did it. We all make decisions and hope that we are doing the best job we can.

Is it even feminist to question how good you are at being a feminist?!

When I first became a feminist, I was also intent on black and white, no gray areas, no excuses. I was very antiporn, in the sense that I looked at all porn stars as sexual victims who needed my help in some way. However, once I started talking to other feminists, I realized that this was a shitty thing to do. To see all porn stars as victims, when not all of them are, is some weirdo "savior shit." There are heavy problems within that industry, but it doesn't mean the women who choose to do it are our enemies.

To be a feminist, it's good to be a champion of women, and generally put one thing above all the rest: the idea that women are allowed to make their own rational, well-thought-out decisions about their lives. If a woman wants to have an abortion,

I want her to have one if that's her sound, reasonable decision. If a porn star gets into the business because she wants to make money and likes sex, and she's totally of sound mind to make this decision for herself, I want the industry she works in to protect her. It's always good to check and make sure that your feminism is inclusive. It's easy to judge the world by your own experiences, but you have to remember that we are all different, and we are all entitled to whatever kind of lifestyle we choose to survive.

This is my feminism. I really do want women to make their own personal choices, and I want those choices to be easy for them to make. For me, it's more disconcerting that there are so many obstacles in a woman's way for her to make those decisions. That's what worries me the most. I'm worried that a woman won't be able to make a decision about her abortion because she's in a state that has few abortion clinics. I'm worried that a woman won't be able to wear a revealing outfit because she'll be screamed at on the way home. I'm worried that a woman won't be able to get the job she deserves because nobody wants to hire an emotional LADY.

I try to be a little more open-minded about things now, because that's the kind of feminism that makes me comfortable. I want my feminism to be one of learning, of growing, and in general, the kind that says, "Let women make their own choices, because dudes get to make their own choices *all the time*."

Saying you're a feminist doesn't mean you are a spokesperson for the entire movement. There are a lot of different ways to be one. You will always be learning. However, if you are curious, the following is a brief cheat sheet, featuring many of the times I've been asked, "Is this feminist?"

Is It Feminist?

To Get Married

I'm starting with this one because it's the question I get asked the absolute most.

I've been in a pretty serious relationship for years with a man, and the more I talk about being a feminist, the more people shove this question in my face.

"Are you guys going to get *married*?!"

If all things go in the direction they are going, sure, considering he still finds me attractive after watching me eat.

"But do feminists get married? Is that okay???"

My answer to them is always this: "Oh, I don't fucking *KNOW*!!!"

I really don't. I've wanted to get married my whole life, before and after I became a feminist. I really like weddings. I want to slap on a retro ivory dress that is short and flares out and is mostly lace on top. I want to do my hair in an updo with a little pearly clip or some autumnal flowers. I want to wear long-lasting red lipstick. I want to have an open bar that some people very much overindulge in. I want to have amazing little appetizers and, frankly, a dinner that leaves a little to be desired. I want to have a fucking party. I want to go on a cool honeymoon. I also want better health care than I currently have, but that's a separate issue. I also like the idea of weddings because I like the idea of committing yourself to a person who is contractually obligated to listen to all the details of your boring day. I'm cheesy, and I love the idea of love and parties and dancing in a dress.

I am aware of the things that make weddings problematic. I'm very aware that a woman who doesn't get married is considered tragic. I don't agree. I love my father very much, so I've never minded the idea of him accompanying me while I strut down the aisle, but I'm not such a fan of how this is called "giving me away." If my father had the option of doing this, he would have probably done it in my teenage years when I was in much worse emotional shape and required much, much more expensive dental work on my parents' dime. What will I do about this? I don't know yet. Maybe he will walk me down the aisle to the audiotape of this book. I think throwing a bouquet in the hopes that it means one of my other friends will marry is not something I jibe with, because I don't care if my friends get married. I probably won't change my name, because I like that people always ask me if I am related to Ted Nugent. I am not, I say, though I'm very certain we would not like each other.

But I don't know. I don't know if I'm doing something evil by getting married, but it certainly doesn't feel like that to me. I want to, and if you want to, you should, too. And if you don't want to, you shouldn't. It's really up to you, and totally your business.

So I don't fucking know, but fall in love, be happy, and stop asking people if they plan on getting married.

To Want to Be Sexy and Girly

Sometimes I dress up to look hot by society's standards. I know what society likes, and sometimes I like to give it to 'em fierce. Straightened hair, a little cleave, some short outfits that show off the gams.

I don't wear things I'm specifically uncomfortable with, but I certainly wear stuff I'm uncomfortable *in*. Every time I slap on a bodycon dress, which is the underwear version of a boa constrictor, it's not because I want to try to switch my liver with my kidneys. That's what it feels like, but it's really because I want to look thinner and wear a tight dress. Every time I put on a pair of high heels, it isn't because I want my feet to feel like I am stabbing them with knives; it's because I want my legs to look longer. I wear push-up bras even though the underwire leaves bright red marks on my skin. I buy tight jeans I have to put on by lying on my bed, pulling with the Jaws of Life. However, I am also willing to acknowledge I don't always do this for myself. I acknowledge that I do this because I like when people tell me I look nice. I like compliments. And I can't go to a birthday dinner wearing my giant shirt of choice—a T-shirt with a cow holding a beer mug on it that says SAVE MILK DRINK BEER. So I put on a little black dress because I know it flatters my ass and I go out.

I also love stereotypically girly shit. I love slathering myself in lotion that smells like a sugar truck slammed into a flower shop. I love painting my nails and buying cupcakes with glitter and bows on them, and I love singing into a microphone to "Genie in a Bottle." I love giggling with my friends and putting on face masks. It feels good. To say that feminists, women who fight for their rights, aren't *allowed* to subscribe to beauty standards when they choose to is a way to distract. It's a way to lure women who take pride in their appearance away from the real issues of feminism. It's idiotic, and it's a lie, and it's dumb. I know plenty of feminists who look great and done up *while* fighting for equality.

So wear a fucking dress if you want to! If you don't want to, don't. Looking nice and dressing up have never made what a feminist is, and never will.

To Like and Enjoy Men

So I get this anecdote a lot: Alice, the maid from *The Brady Bunch*, once lived in what was potentially a lesbian commune. People tell me this story like perhaps it's what I would like to do, too. That maybe because I am a feminist I would like to live in a world that doesn't have any men at all.

I am not saying this is a particularly awful thing, probably. If there were a commune where women could go and never see khaki cargo shorts, I think that would be a pretty nice thing. And if there weren't any Hooters restaurants. And if there were all these different kinds of frozen-yogurt places, and if there were sports bars we could go to without things getting weird, and if there were only bathrooms for women. And if there were twice the number of hummus places and we'd all just get very comfortable and friendly, and we could just lie around and chat and learn different kinds of braids.

I'm not saying that it's specifically what I want above all things. I just like the idea of maybe never being interrupted, and perhaps being able to go topless in public if I needed to, say, get a Fanta at the store. I'm saying that that would also be *a very nice thing*. I like having sex with men, but I still think this would be a *very nice thing*.

I also happen to really like men. Some of my best friends are men! Their T-shirts and razors are absolutely fantastic. I like hanging out with them and joking around with them, and hearing about how they are sometimes scared of women. Men aren't the enemy. Some of them are misogynists, but not all of them. I don't immediately trust them, but I have some amazing male friends I like to chill with. I'm very tired of the idea that men and women can't be friends. I'm very tired of hearing that we are so different from each other. I'm very tired that our genders define us in such a way that we're different and incompatible as buddies. I'm not here to demonize men, but I am here to make sure they treat me with respect. That's really all. If they do, I'll have a beer or two with them.

As long as they keep their unwanted dick pics to themselves, treat me as respectfully as I will them, and don't use the word "friendzone" around me, I have no ill will toward them.

To Like Kim Kardashian

If you think becoming a billionaire by taking a bunch of photos of yourself isn't badass, think again. If you think getting on the cover of *Vogue* isn't badass, despite people reminding you every single day you are just a whore who released a sex tape, think again. If you don't like her, whatever, but let me tell you: owning a bunch of businesses and being a sex symbol who wears the tightest most form-fitting clothes on the planet, all while hanging out with your family 24/7, is probably not the easiest gig.

But just so you know: I'm Team Amber Rose all the way.

To Watch Porn

I'm not a big porn watcher. I have a very vivid imagination and an excellent memory. For instance, I can recall every detail of the most romantic and sexual night I ever spent with the cast of *X-Men: Days of Future Past*. I can remember how Hugh Jackman *was not there*. I can remember that Michael Fassbender was *definitely there*. On a side note, I am very sexually terrified by Michael Fassbender, even in my fantasies. So.

I'm also not into porn because I don't have the time and the patience to find a video that makes me excited enough to grab at myself. If I had four hours to search, maybe I would have more of a go at it, but I'm a busy woman as it is (kind of).

My main issue? Most porn isn't for women. Women can *legally watch it*, but it's definitely not for them. Porn seems to forget that women actually enjoy sex enough to want to watch it on camera. I'm interested in it. You can see all the weird spins and thrusts you would never try at home. You can watch things you aren't necessarily ready to try, like butt things. You can watch things you would *never* try, like group sex, because where would you keep your purse and how does one start an orgy? Do you have wine first? Who makes the first move?

Porn is not for women in the way sports and video games are not for women: we like it, we consume it, we're an interested demographic, but everybody tells us we shouldn't, and we don't, and we make it for *men*! Going on a porn site as a woman is also like going to a crap retail store and being plus-sized: here's a tiny section devoted to you that has nothing you like. Good luck! We hate you!

You go to a porn site, and there are forty billion videos with titles like "Blonde Slut Gets Hammered" of some dude ramming it into some lady. Every video description is "slutty teen" or "brunette slore" or "big stupid idiot gets her lady parts drilled and we HATE HER." Porn, specifically mainstream porn, dismisses me.

Most women don't want to see other women get *so excited* at the sight of a dick they have to rip all their polyester clothing off. We want a medium amount of realistic excitement at the dick. We don't want to look at it as a present. Most women want to have lesbian sex like adults, instead of as two twenty-two-year-old "teens" at their stepmother's sleepover. Women don't have to be props. They can be participants.

I don't think porn is evil. I think porn is a flawed industry.

I think the bad parts of the porn industry are incredibly insidious, and the more we respect the women who participate in it, the more we can start to change those insidious things. I think women are starting to say they watch porn. I think if you do watch porn, you should say you watch porn. I think we need to get everybody on the same page of comfort: we watch it, but we will watch it more if it doesn't suck.

I am also aware of the way we talk about porn. All the people who have told me they have watched porn have also mentioned, at some point, how a lot of porn stars are drug addicts and come from bad homes and how gross porn stars all are and all that jazz. I think we feel very guilty about watching porn because (a) we still think sex is kind of dirty and (b) we know some porn isn't ethical, but we don't know which films. Sex is not dirty. A lot of people watch porn. So we need to make sex work safe for the women and men who choose to be in the industry. We need to make sure that all the men and women who are in the industry are paid for their time, that their acts are consensual, that they are protected from disease, and that they are of legal age. I'd like to see people treat sex work like a real job, with the confidence that the people who do this type of work do so because they really want to do it.

When that happens? Maybe I'll start watching porn. *But that's just my own thing.* A lot of women I know are uncomfortable watching porn, and I get that. There are plenty of important arguments to be made against it. However, you can also watch porn if you genuinely want to, because you are a sexual being and it's fine to act on your urges. If you want to be particularly socially conscious, hit Google and research porn companies that seem to treat their employees with respect, or companies that are geared toward the female experience. If that's too much Google and you're itching to slap at your privates, all I ask is that you think of porn stars as human beings, and consume the porn that makes them all seem as such. Like, maybe move on if the video is called "Shaved Slut Party." It's the very least you can do for porn stars' services.

Then go get your freak on, clean yourself up, and don't call your mother for at least an hour after you're done.

To Talk Shit About Other Women

I believe very strongly in sisterhood. I believe in giving the women who come into your life a chance. I believe in not shutting other women out before giving them a chance.

I also believe very strongly that some people are the worst. I am not excluding other women in this because I'm a feminist, either. I give men and women equal treatment when it comes to characteristics I hate. Unfortunately, that list is pretty long: people who are intolerant, people who touch your shoulders or stand too close to you when they talk, people who are rude, people who talk about Paleo more than other topics, people who hate dogs, bad tippers, people who make offhand comments about popular television and music because they are *so cool*, people who say "girly" like it's a bad word, guys who wear tiny animals on their shorts but are also adults, people who say, "Have you been to Europe?" and then make a face when you say no, people who complain about their food too much, people who talk about exercising a lot, guys who keep injecting *articles* they read into the conversation, people who say you look tired. There's more, but I also don't like people who make very long lists.

Talking shit about people can be very relaxing. There isn't anything better than leaving a party with a friend and just blasting off a monologue about how horrible you thought

Miranda was because she kept asking everybody for a bite of their sandwich even though she was "not hungry enough to eat." Miranda, for one, always does this. She always says she's not hungry even though I know she is. Then, she asks for bites of *your food*, but she takes two bites of yours even though she says she will only take one. Then, there's Jen. Jen always comes up to *you* at parties, but expects you to lead the conversation. She just kind of stares at you until you bring topics up, and she's never enthusiastic about it.

They are nice people, but they are horrible to talk to sometimes, and the only respite I have is going back to my other friends and complaining about everyone. I have friendships based around complaining about mutual friends. I am Olympia Dukakis in *Steel Magnolias* in this way: "If you have nothing nice to say, come sit by me."

You can do this in a very restrained, feminist-approved way. You can talk about how somebody sucks big-time without using the words we know are harmful: slut, whore, fat, stupid, bitch. Just rely very heavily on all the horrible things about her that are specific: like how she keeps talking about how excited she is to come to your party and then never shows up to your party.

I believe women need to support each other. I also don't believe in giving women any special flowery treatment, where I have to be nice to them all the time because they are women. Therefore, I believe very heartily in talking shit about people who deserve it, sometimes.

To Be a Stay-at-Home Mother

Oh, please. The idea that wanting to be a housewife, a mother, or any other "traditional" role for women is something a feminist doesn't believe in is kind of nuts. If there were no mothers, there would be no children. I've seen *Children of Men* at least 1.5 times. I know a world with no children is absolute chaos. *Wanting* to be anything is the whole point of feminism. *Having to be something* is what feminists fight against, or at least the ones I know. Being barefoot in the kitchen at a young age with a baby is not an ideal state for anyone. That used to be the norm in the 1950s, a decade people still surprisingly revere even though it was a racist, shitty time period. Like, I know people are just idolizing the fifties *aesthetic*, rather than the lack of civil liberties, but still. I suggest wearing some cat eyeliner and a sweater set in 2015, a time where it's not legal to kick people out of a restaurant because of their color.

For some reason, since I've seen the #womenagainstfeminism hashtag, wanting to be a mother is associated with not being a feminist. It's ridiculous. It's wrong. Make your own choices, people. Pop out babies and stay home if you want to. I work from home all the time and the honest-to-God truth is I never want to leave my house again. I'm hoping to work, be a mother, and eventually die on my couch, in sweatpants.

To Not Be Inclusive

If you think transwomen are not women, then you are not the kind of feminist I hang around with. Period. End of story.

It is also important to be aware of all the issues that don't directly affect you. There's a whole world out there of women struggling much worse than you, now. I suggest you start educating yourself on all of them. While there are many hurdles the women you know have to face, there are many who face much worse. Just keep that in mind.

To Scream at Everyone

If you consider yourself a feminist, you don't have to post on Facebook every day about it. You don't have to post wild accusations, either, like NO MEN SHOULD EVEN LOOK AT ME or whatever. You don't have to shove people out the window because they make a joke at a party that has the word "women" in it. It would be nice to keep up with issues, and to start conversations when you notice problematic behavior, or not to laugh when people make a stupid joke. But you do not have to go CAPS LOCK on the world. You can relax.

To Have Men Open Jars for You

Opening jars is often cited when talking about chivalry. Without men, ladies would never be able to enjoy a caper with some lox, drop a pimiento olive into an already busy salad, or spread whole-grain mustard on a ham sandwich. Men opened jars for us, we all nodded one day, and we went with it. I have heard people be very passionate about this, fresh spittle punctuating the air: "Wha . . . wha . . . can't men just OPEN jars for women without women screaming about being independent? Can't a man just be chivalrous without getting *attacked*?"

My response to this is *sure*. Open the fucking jar for me. I sure can't. Recently, I tried to open a jar of roasted red peppers to put a slice on leftover white pizza. It would have been delicious. It would have made my whole meal less sad. But I couldn't do it. I ran it under hot water; I put rubber bands on it; I considered shattering it and rubbing blood on the walls with the words "No Jars May Enter Here." I had my pizza with *nothing on it that night*. One day, I might be able to open up a jar, and then I promise you a very important thing will happen: men will no longer exist.

The real question at hand: Can anyone *really* open a jar? Is opening up a jar even possible *for men*? In all my years as a person, I've had probably around three jars opened in my presence. My roommates and I once passed around a jar of pickles for about twenty minutes before the seal popped, and we munched on them greedily, with red hands.

So, yes. It's perfectly fine to have a man or anybody in your presence attempt to open a jar for you. They'll try for four seconds and then they will hand it back to you. Sometimes it will open, sometimes it will not, sometimes you'll have to eat the pizza without the toppings, and eventually we will all die.

There are three truths you need to remember as a feminist: (1) You are allowed to shift beliefs and be wrong and learn. There are times you will realize you were part of the problem, and the best you could do is correct your behavior and acknowledge that. (2) If you were so strict that you never did anything problematic or watched anything problematic or listened to anything problematic ever again, you would have to sit in a room with yellow wallpaper for the rest of your life. We live in a patriarchal society, babies. This stuff is *everywhere*. (3) There is no one singular kind of woman.

Being a feminist means one thing to me: it means letting women make decisions for themselves, and women having the opportunities and the equal playing field it takes in order to make those decisions for themselves. To me, everything else is just noise.

The real answer to "Is it feminist?" should always be: "I

don't know. Did you make the decision of your own accord? Are you judging somebody by your own beliefs, or letting her make decisions according to her own experiences and world-views?"

That's when you have your answer. Sometimes the answer is yes. Sometimes it is no. And sometimes, you just gotta shake your head, smile, and keep on dancing to a terrible song.

And One More Thing

My best friend sent me a link to an Internet list the other day. It was some millennial crap I constantly read and always, at this point, sort of detest. "20 Ways You Know You Are in Your Late 20s," maybe. "20 Reasons Girls Stay Home on a Friday Night." I don't know. They are all so similar: women our age like to stay in; we like to watch television shows and eat ice cream and paint our nails and think about Tina Fey. The true modern woman, living her youth with the world at her fingertips, but mostly, she's just on the Internet, sitting in her pajamas.

I never want to leave the house that much anymore. Sometimes, the world seems too difficult for me to want to maneuver. There's so much to think about: Do I want to take the route home that is the safest or the shortest? Do I want to be spoken at rather than to? Do I want to wear that skirt, knowing I'll hear comments about it? Other times, I just want to sit in the apartment I pay a little bit too much for. Either way, I understand it. I read the lists, and I feel some sort of camaraderie in the world.

My friend jokes: "How did our mothers learn to grow up without *lists*?!"

She is kidding. Still, I think, I am close to my mother's age when she was raising me. She grew up in a world considerably different than mine. When I was born, she didn't know what it would be like for a girl in the world. She wondered how I would land gracefully, or if I would be hurt, or if I would even have a shot.

The world is a scary, scary place, but I sure as hell have a *shot*. I'm twenty-six now, and I feel the voice I have earned in this world deserves to be heard. Not everyone knows they have a voice; not everyone knows they have choices, but I do. My mother was born in a time when there was no *Roe v. Wade*. My grandmother was born in a world where people didn't feel women should *vote*. There is a common thread, though.

We are all fighters.

Women have always been fighters. I know this because the world is different than it used to be. I have more opportunities than I would have had before. Things have changed.

I still know it isn't safe to be a woman in this world. I still believe we are looking behind us, wherever we go. We speak loudly, even under the threat of consequences. We know the consequences, and we fear them. Sometimes, because of them, we stay quiet. We stay quiet because we want people to like us, because we are not used to speaking.

Sometimes, we speak up. This is our revolution. This is our fight: it's us, speaking up for ourselves. Just as it was before, just as it always will be.

I try not to say the phrase "strong woman" anymore, because I think it's almost redundant at this point. Women have iron in their bones. Women grit their teeth and bear it. Women rise up. A strong woman is *any* woman. Sometimes it's me, and sometimes it's you.

I don't know if I've convinced you to be a feminist. I don't know if you read this book feeling empowered enough to use the voice you were given. I believe feminism is about choice and is ultimately *a choice to make. I want you to make all the choices you can, for the rest of your life. I want you to make those choices freely.* No matter what you think about me or my feminism, or what anybody thinks about me, for that matter.

I make the choice to be a feminist because I feel like I have to. I make that choice not because I hate men, or love men, or feel anything about men at all. I make that choice because I love myself. I make that choice because I respect other women. I make that choice because when I'm older, I will look at the younger generation of women and remember the fights they no longer have to fight, and know my voice wasn't silent on those issues. I make that choice as a flawed woman. I make that choice as someone who wants to learn. I make that choice as a woman who knows that feminism is not perfect. I make that choice with women who know their lives might change today for the worse, because the world is still a dangerous place for them. I make that choice with women who want to shake the very foundations of a system that views them differently than they see themselves. I make that choice, every day. I make that choice because I walk home with my keys in my hand, and so do all the women I know.

And yet:

We still leave the house.

Acknowledgments

This book is for all the girls who inspire me. The girls who struggle and still get up in the morning, the girls who shine in the darkest places, the girls with amazing eyebrows, the girls with big hopes, the girls who blossom and change and grow. It's for the girls who make noise, who tell their stories, who are scared, who fight, who are vulnerable, who are honest, who have more fire and light in their eyes than I ever knew could exist. To the girls who have made me feel so proud to be a girl myself, who redefine the word every day, and who keep me learning. You always give me something to strive for.

This is also for all the muses in my life. These include Dolly Parton, Mindy Kaling, Meryl Streep, and Gilda Radner. To all the television shows I binged on while furiously trying to finish this book: *Orphan Black*, *Gilmore Girls*, *Parenthood*, and late-night Food Network shows. To all the female artists I jammed to while trying to edit this book for the fiftieth time: Kacey Musgraves, Nicki Minaj, Beyoncé, Rihanna, Taylor Swift, Mariah Carey, and Sara Bareilles. Thanks to all the ladies of history and the present who write and inspire and sing and shout for giving me the juju I needed to work my ass off on this book.

Of course, I am lucky enough to actually *know* some of my muses: to Kate Napolitano, my editor and friend. You have pushed me harder than anyone I've ever met, and you are a goddess for dealing with my loose interpretation of deadlines. I'm so lucky to witness your talent and even get to benefit from it, too. To Alyssa Reuben, my agent who trusts me enough to always let me write what I believe in. To Milena Brown, my publicist. To everyone else at Plume and Paradigm for putting their faith in me. To my darling and beautiful mother, who is my rock, my role model, and my inspiration because she looks ten years younger than she actually is. To my brother, for being a wise guy sometimes and a good guy always. To my dad. To my grandmothers, Aida and Mildred. To Max, who only had a slight reference in the last acknowledgments but now gets a name in this one. You have given me so much joy. Thanks for that, my love, and also for letting me ask questions during *Game of Thrones.* To Amanda, my platonic soul mate and dear friend . . . I told you that you were my muse! To Adam and Jimmy, for letting me drink too much in your apartment and gossip at you.

To the readers of *The Frenemy*, my Tumblr, and the first book. To wine, tacos, and MAC Diva lipstick for keeping me sane. To my aunt Peggy, Aunt Linda, Fred, and Titi Vicky, for their constant support and complete willingness to name-drop my book in any conversation they have with strangers. To all my wonderful friends who still like me even after I disappear during crunch time: one day, I'll be rich enough to buy you all drinks (do not hold me to this). To Kat and Kris, for being great cheerleaders. To Sarah and Corey, who let me be in their wedding even though I had to hand in my final draft the very next week. To Louie, who is the best dog.

And to anyone who reads this book, I thank you from the bottom of my heart. Especially if you *like* it.